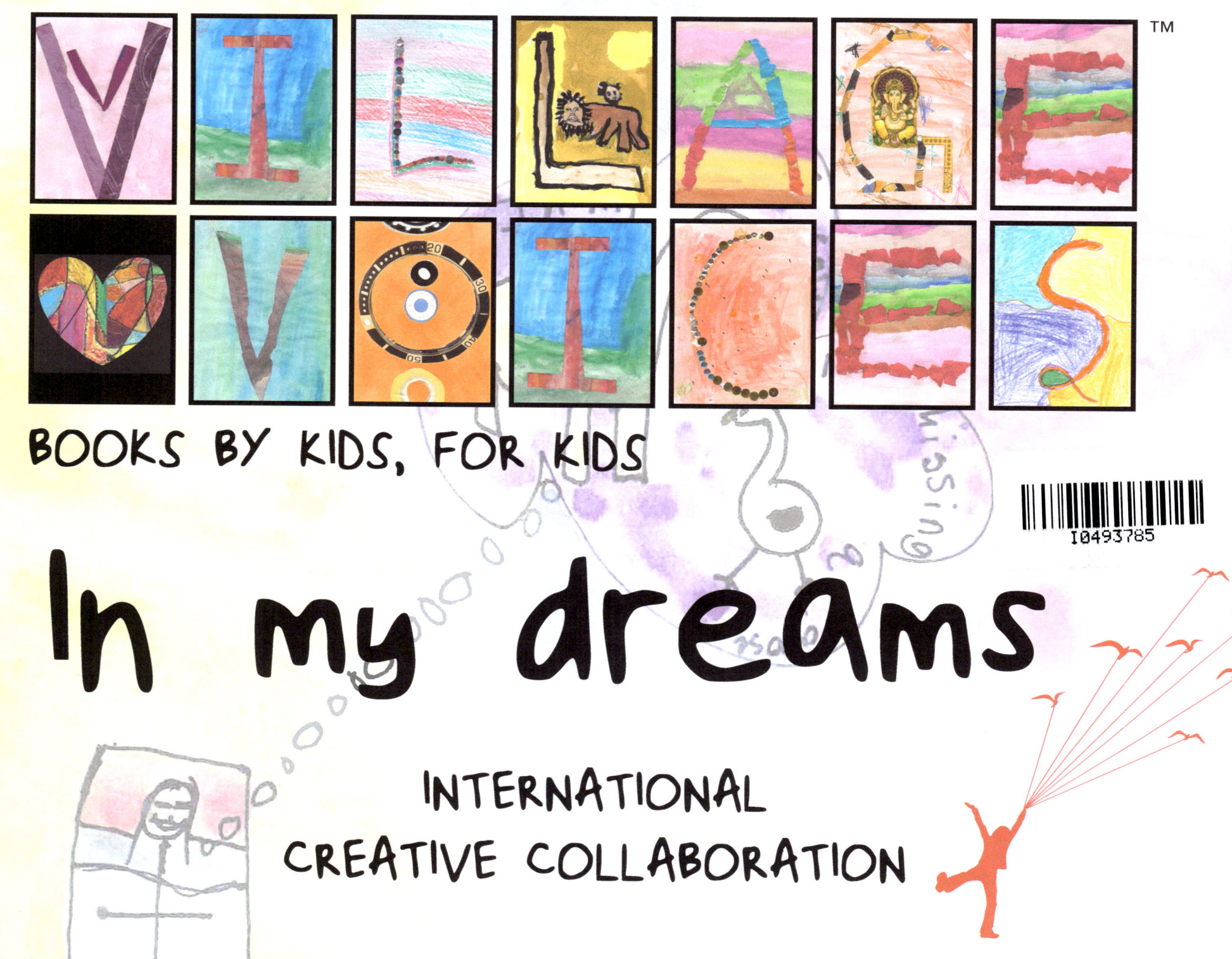

VILLAGE VOICES

BOOKS BY KIDS, FOR KIDS

In my dreams

INTERNATIONAL CREATIVE COLLABORATION

I0493785

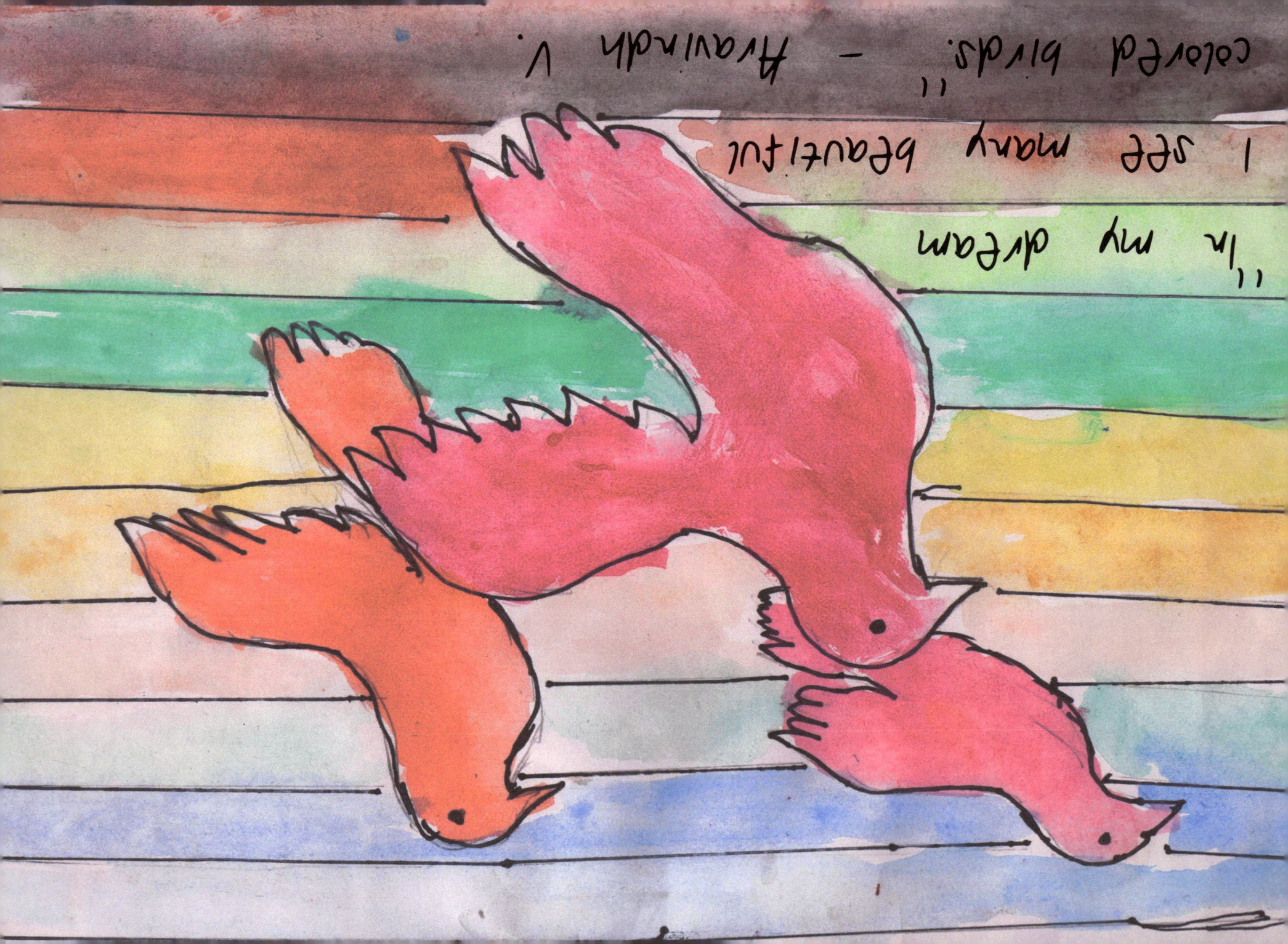

"In my dream
I see many beautiful
colored birds." — Aravindh V.

NEW MOON BOOKS
is an imprint of Salt River Publishing
Phoenix, Arizona
www.SaltRiverPublishing.com

First edition 2017
18 17 16   3 2 1   iii ii i
ISBN: 978-1535582919

Cover art by Azzie
Art editing by Kartik Gera

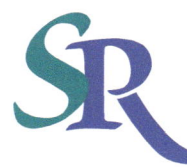

Publisher discount available
SaltRiverPublishing.com/estore/

Art Therapy (Integral Art) provides a VOICE where one may or may not exist…

I dedicate VILLAGE VOICES to children of all ages… May they be blessed with a voice, a vision, the divine light of creativity, self-expression, a love of books and reading.

"Never forget the goal.

Never stop aspiring.

Never halt in your progress, and you will succeed."

The Mother

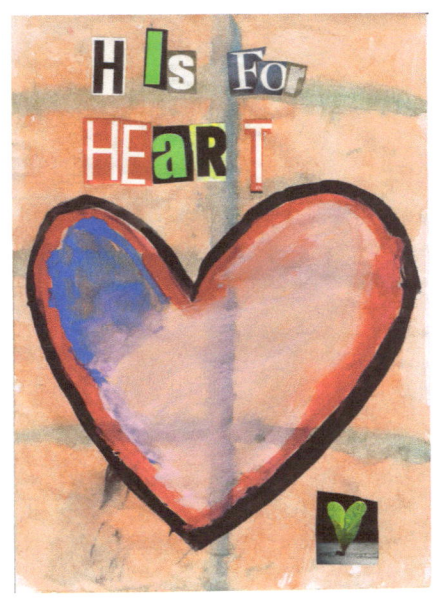

TIA PLEIMAN

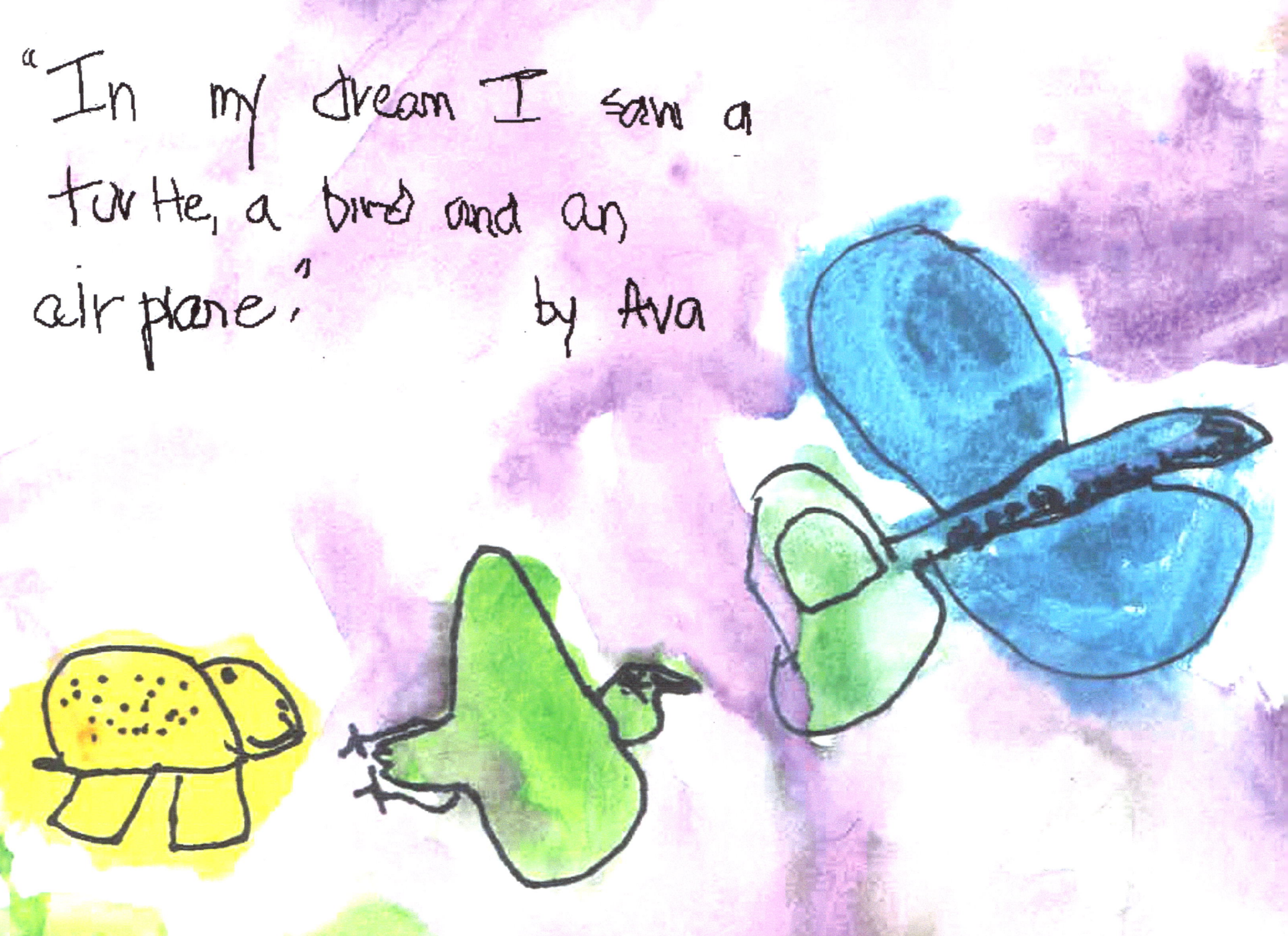

"In my dream I saw a turtle, a bird and an airplane."   by Ava

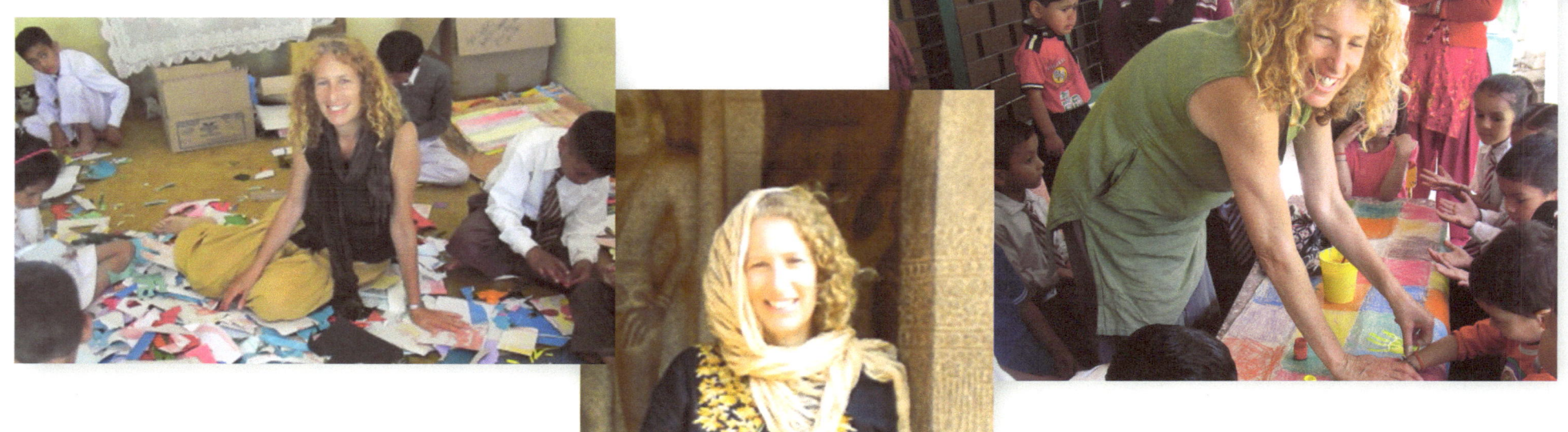

"Village Voices" is a series of books created by village children of all ages. The focus is on Art and Literacy – the result is creative empowerment. The intention of Village Voices is to nurture creativity and self-expression and to inspire a joy for reading.

The project and programs are facilitated by Tia Pleiman, MA, an international art therapist from the USA with 25 years of art therapy and educational experience. For the past 8 years, Tia has been working with urban and village children in north and south India and Nepal.
Tia is passionately committed to facilitating personal growth and development of children, youth and adults through Art Therapy. The tools of transformation are: The philosophies and practice of Integral Education combined with Art Therapy (Integral Art), which serve as the foundation for social, emotional and intellectual development through creative expression, self-reflection, literacy and peace building skills on both an individual and collective level.

THANK YOU for purchasing Village Voices, books by kids for kids. You are helping to support Create and Transform, providing community-based, grassroots Art and Literacy programs and projects, as well as the young authors, artists and schools they attend.

Facebook: Art Therapy with Create and Transform
www.createandtransform.org
tialovesart@gmail.com

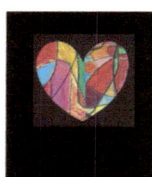

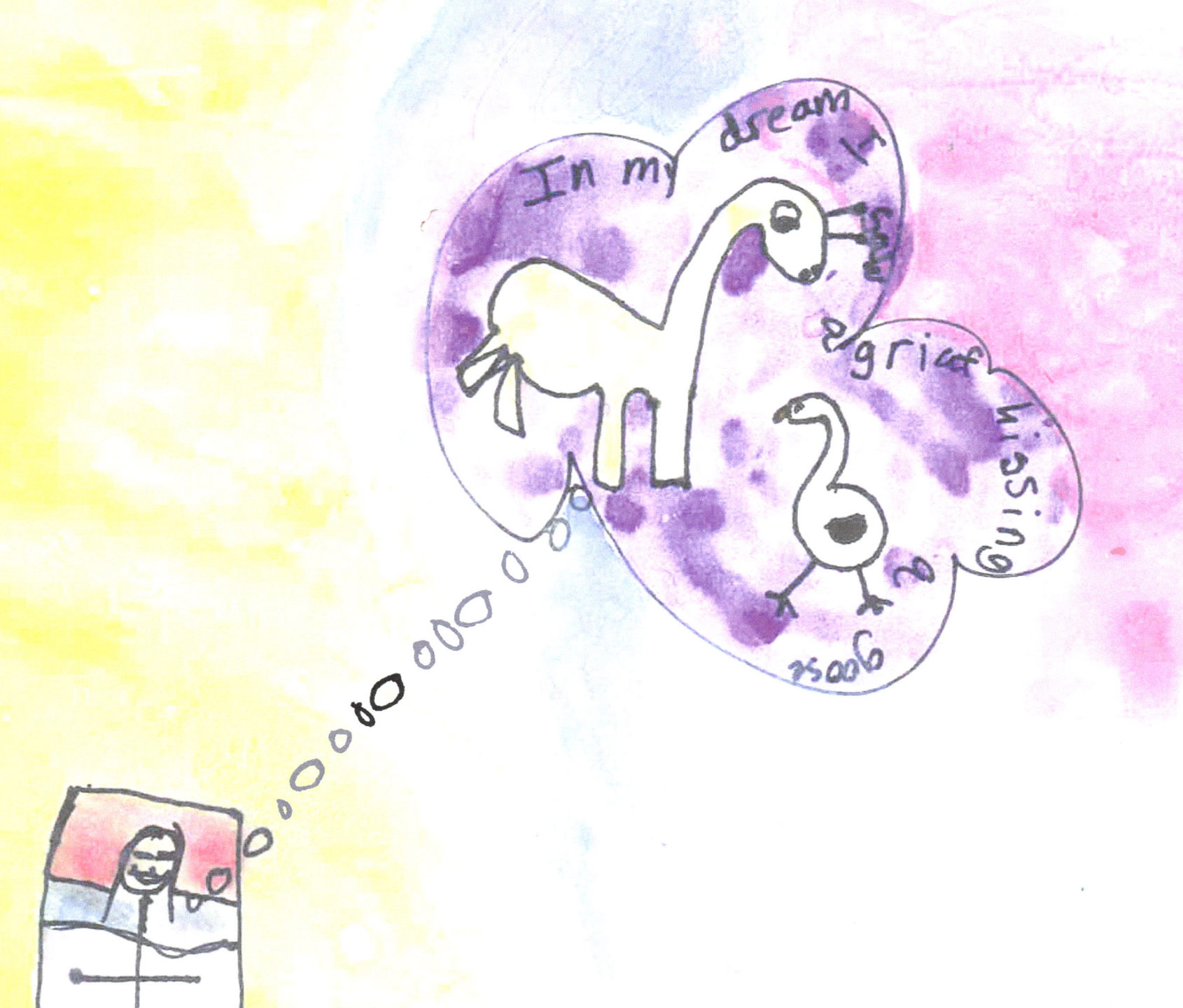

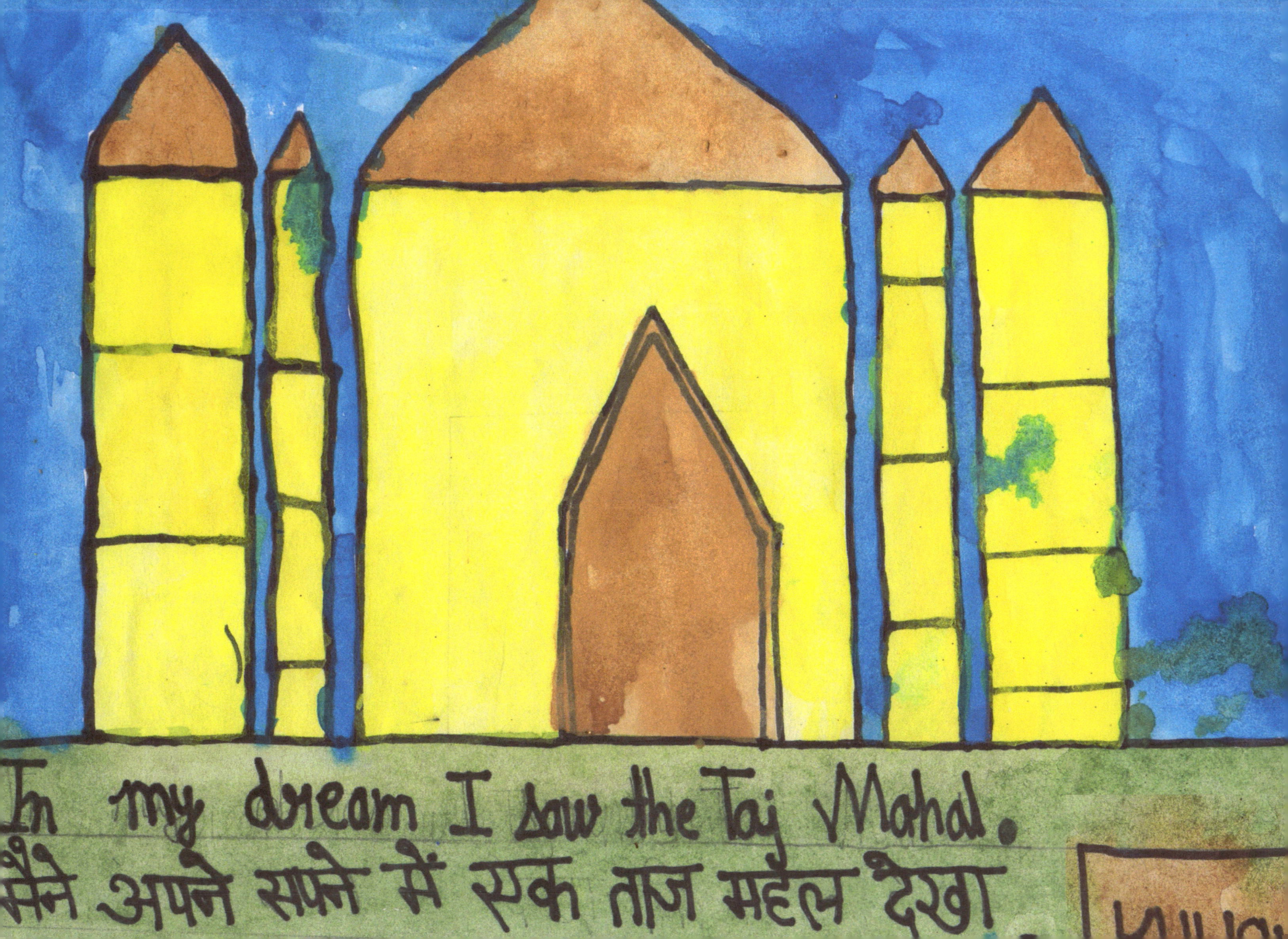

In my dream I saw the Taj Mahal.

मैंने अपने सपने में एक ताज महल देखा।

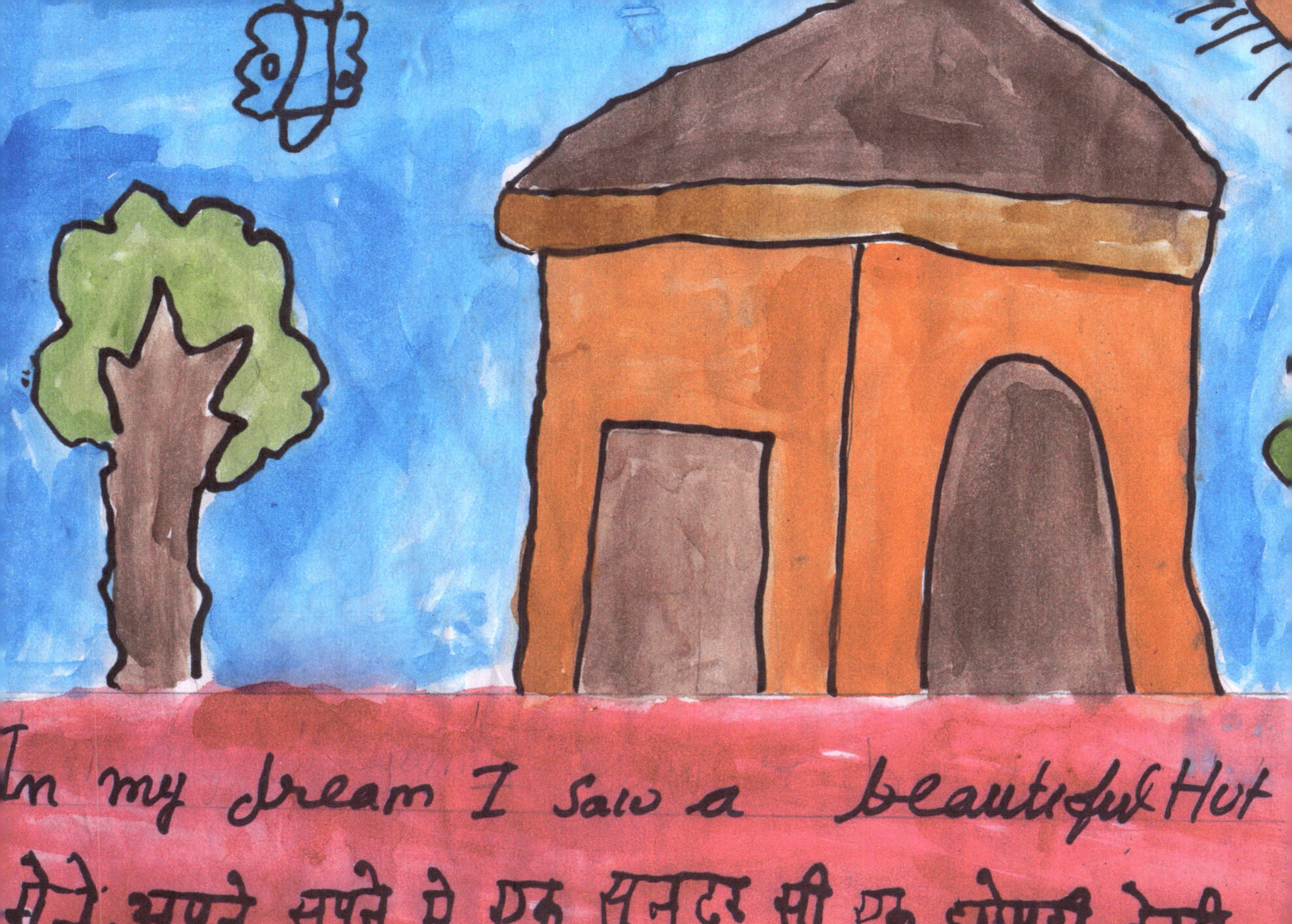

In my dream I saw a beautiful Hut

मेरे अपने सपने मे एक सुन्दर सी एक झोपड़ी हैमी

In My Dream   I See Lion
and I runaway and I See Monkey Also
and I See Sun also.

मेरो सपनामा मैंले सिंह देख्यो ! र म भागेँ, र बाँदर न देख्यो र सूर्य पनि देख्यो !

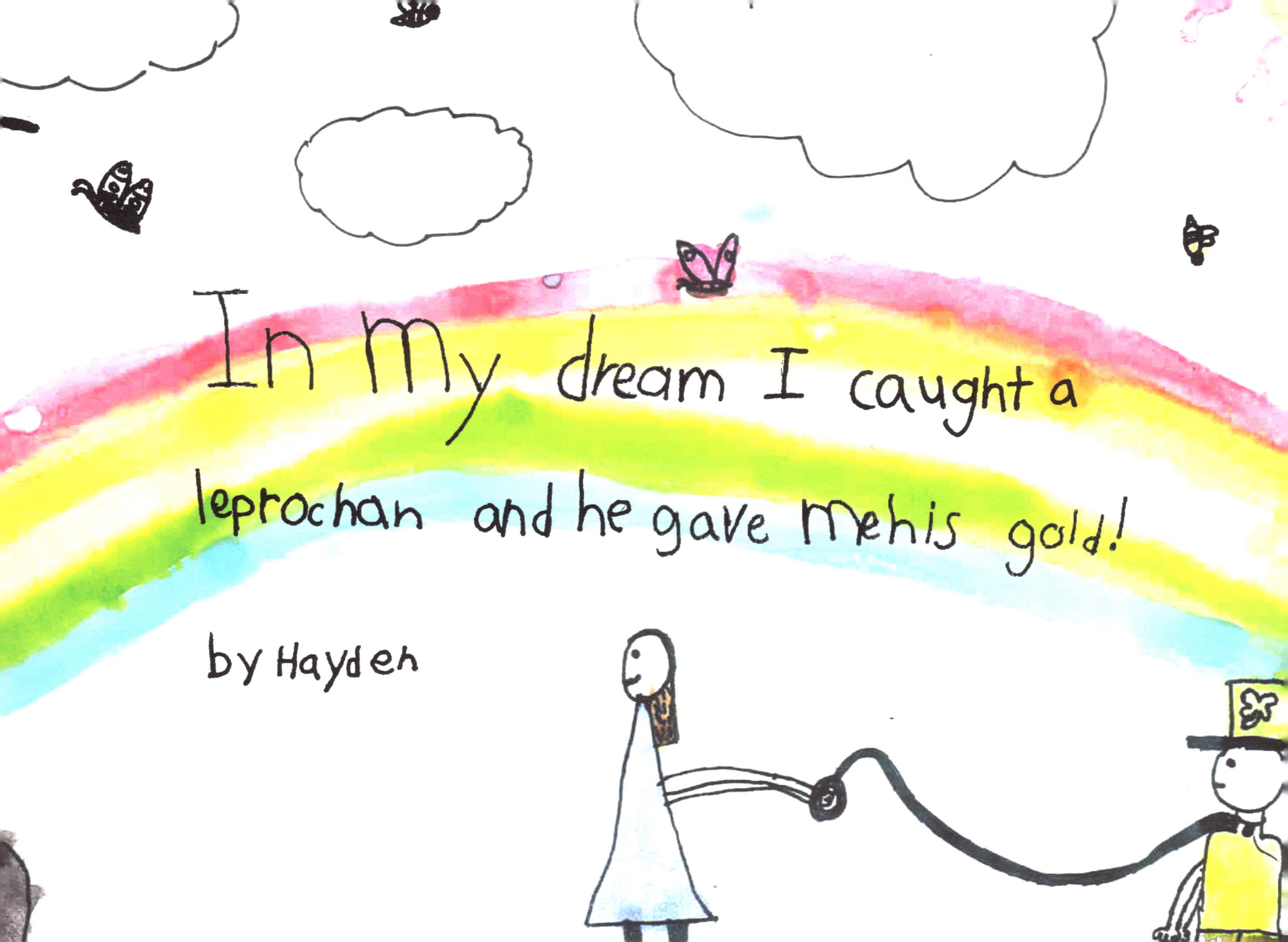

In my dream I caught a leprochan and he gave me his gold!

by Hayden

I dream to see a moon fairy on the perfect date ever. The moon will be right next to the fairy. And then a shooting star will just pass by.

— Azzie

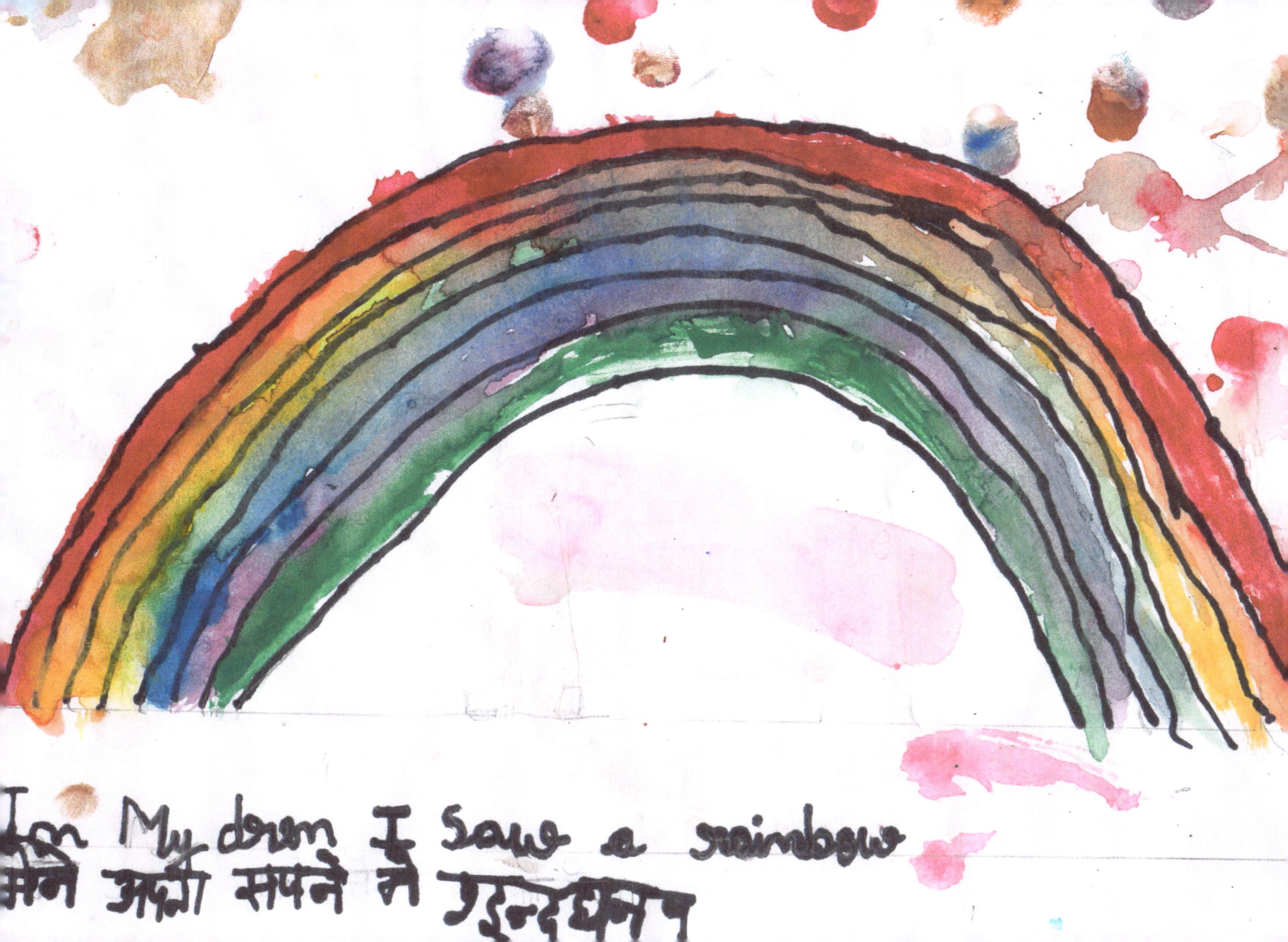

In My dream I Saw a rainbow

मैंने अपने सपने में इन्द्रधनुष

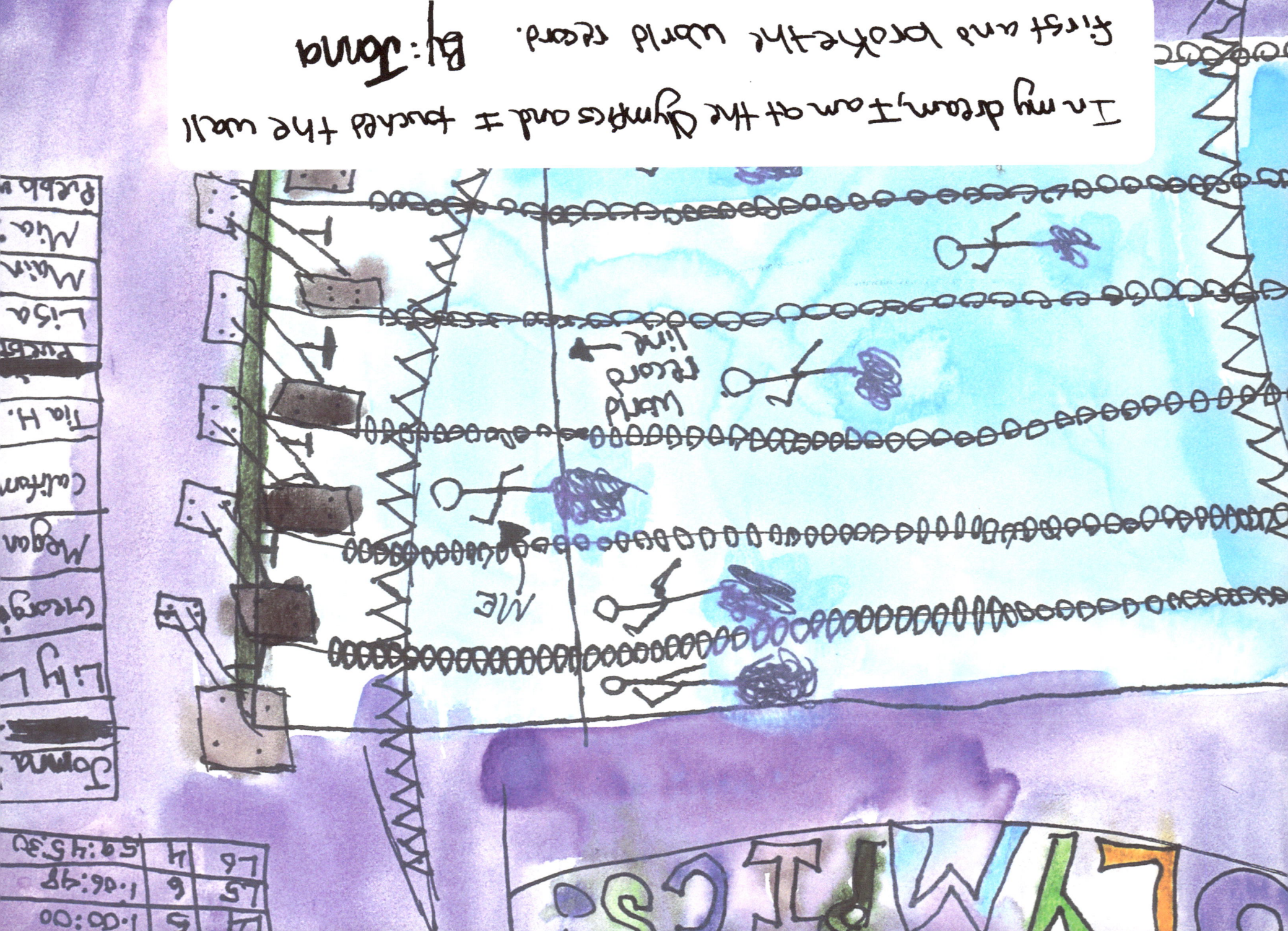

In my dream, I am at the Olympics and I broke the wall
first and broke the world record. By: Jona

World record line

ME

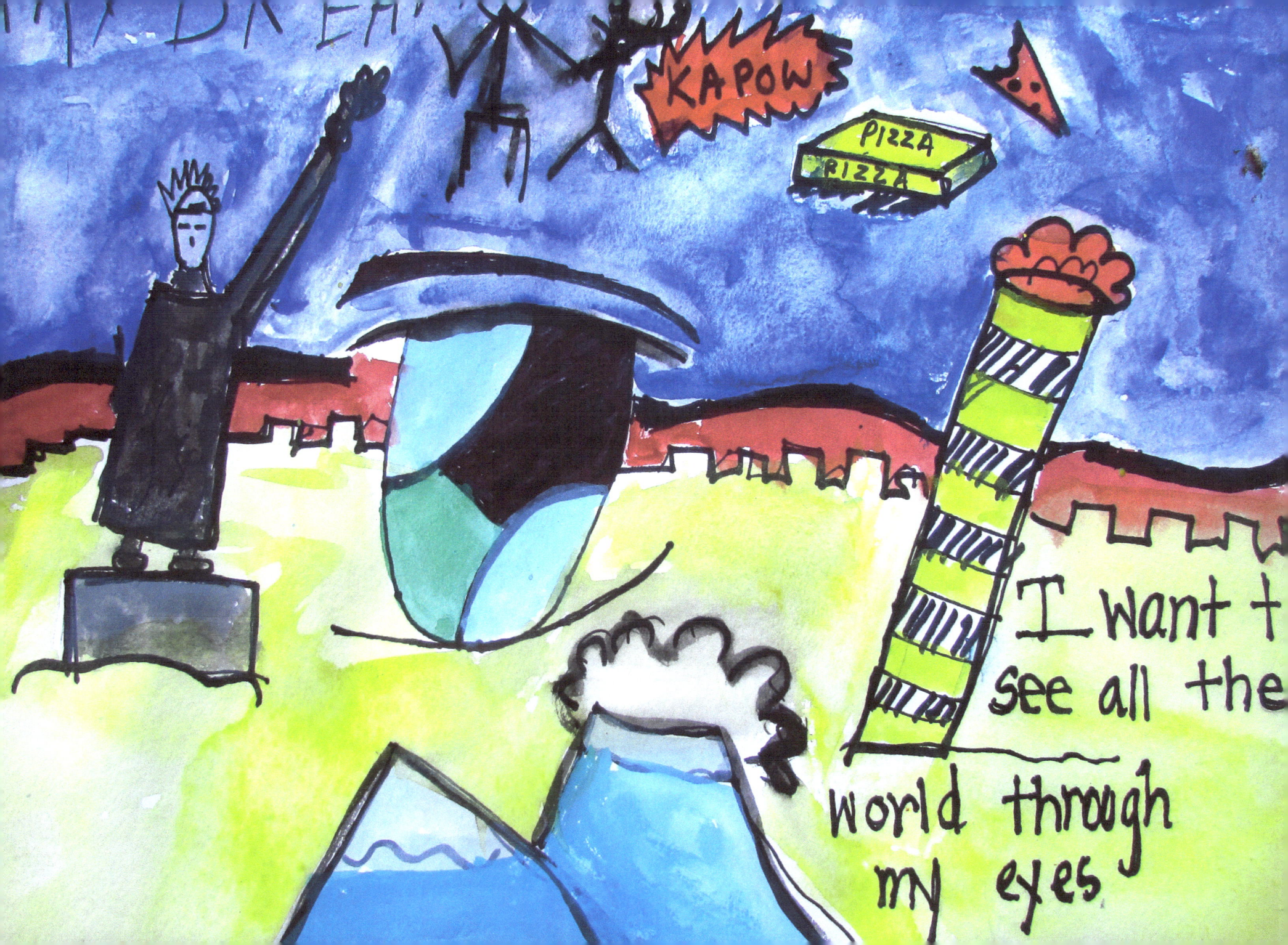

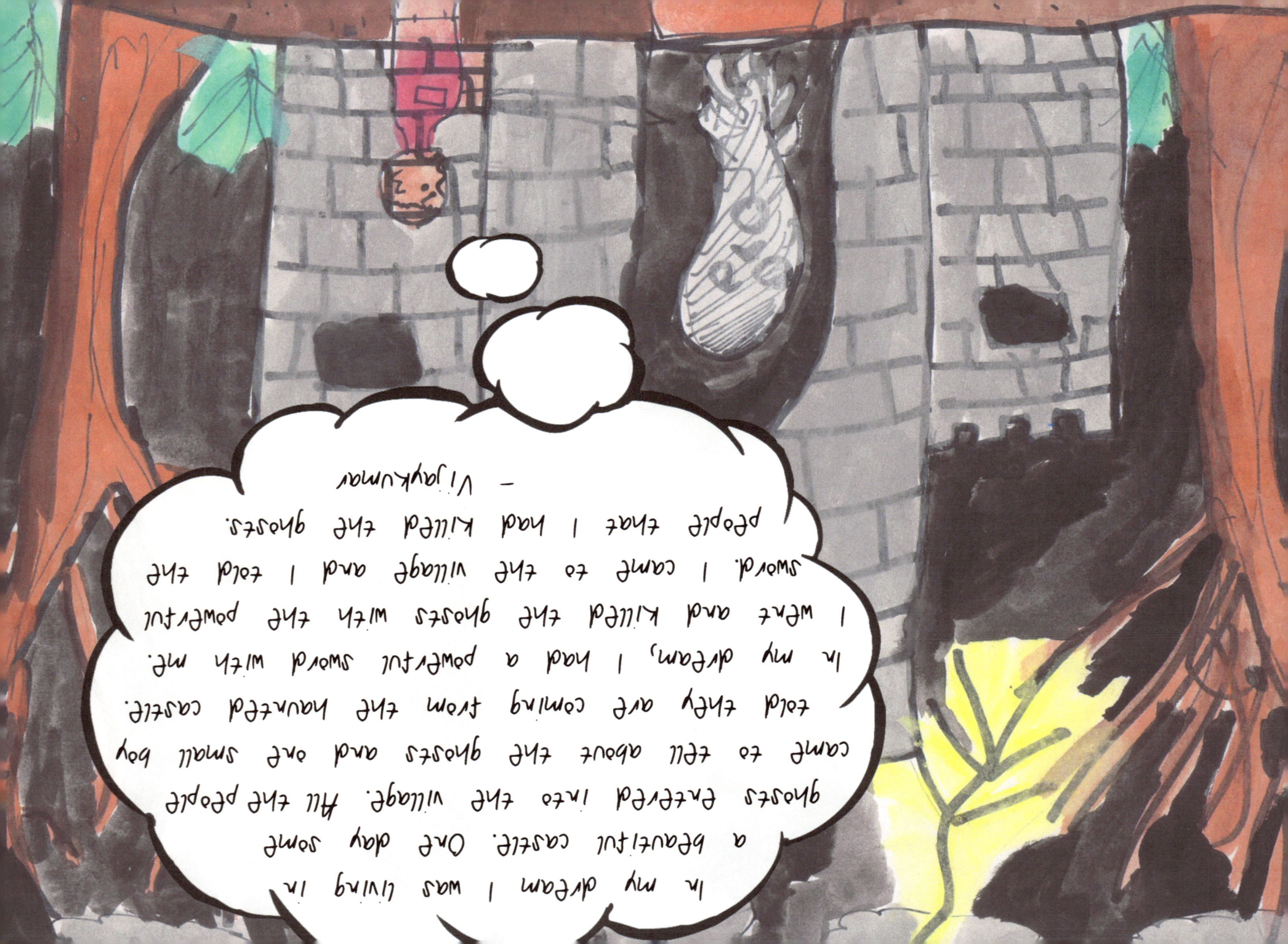

In my dream I was living in
a beautiful castle. One day some
ghosts entered into the village. All the people
came to tell about the ghosts and one small boy
told they are coming from the haunted castle.
In my dream, I had a powerful sword with me.
I went and killed the ghosts with the powerful
sword. I came to the village and I told the
people that I had killed the ghosts.

— Vijaykumar

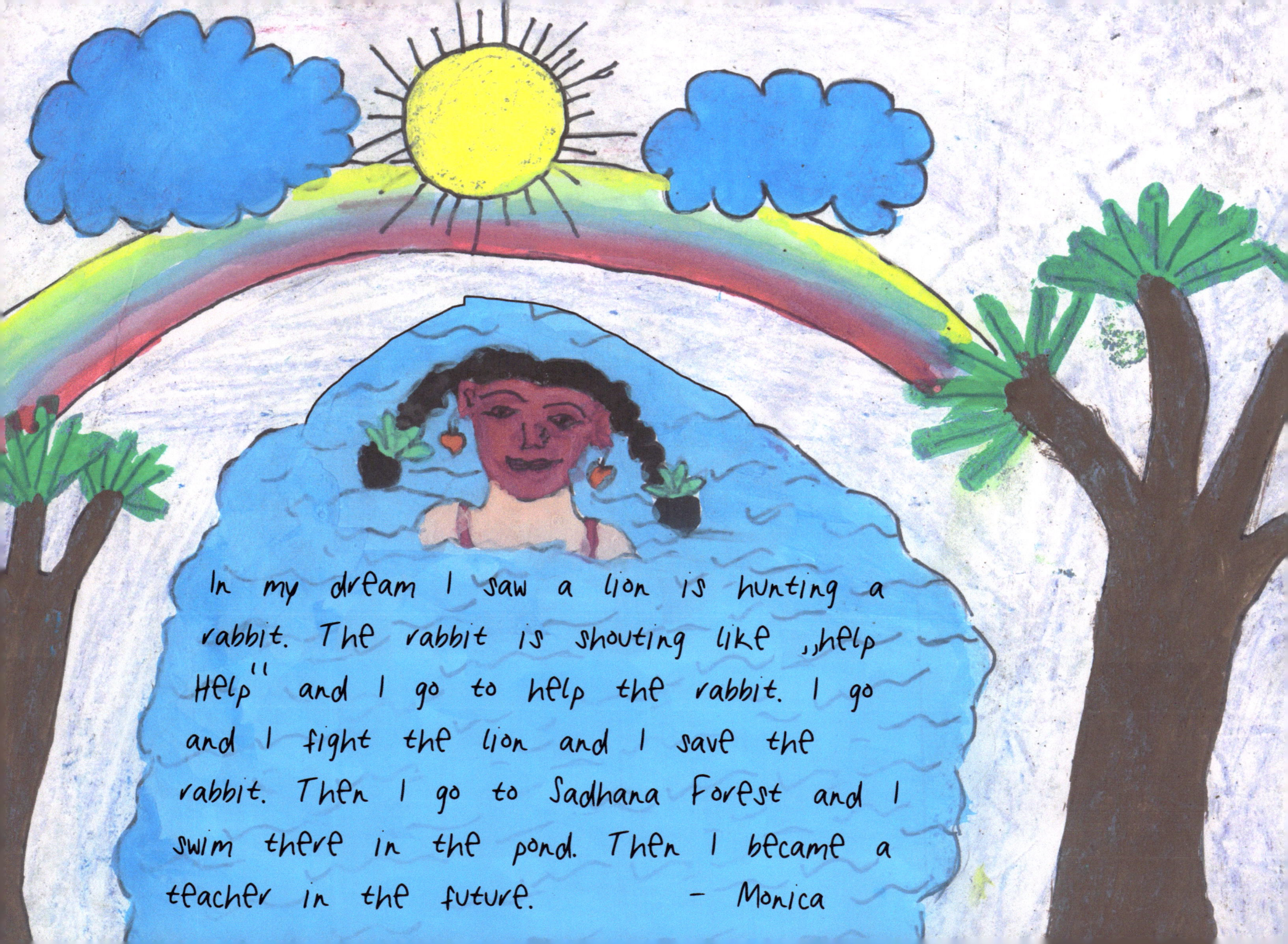

In my dream I saw a lion is hunting a rabbit. The rabbit is shouting like ,,help Help'' and I go to help the rabbit. I go and I fight the lion and I save the rabbit. Then I go to Sadhana Forest and I swim there in the pond. Then I became a teacher in the future.   – Monica

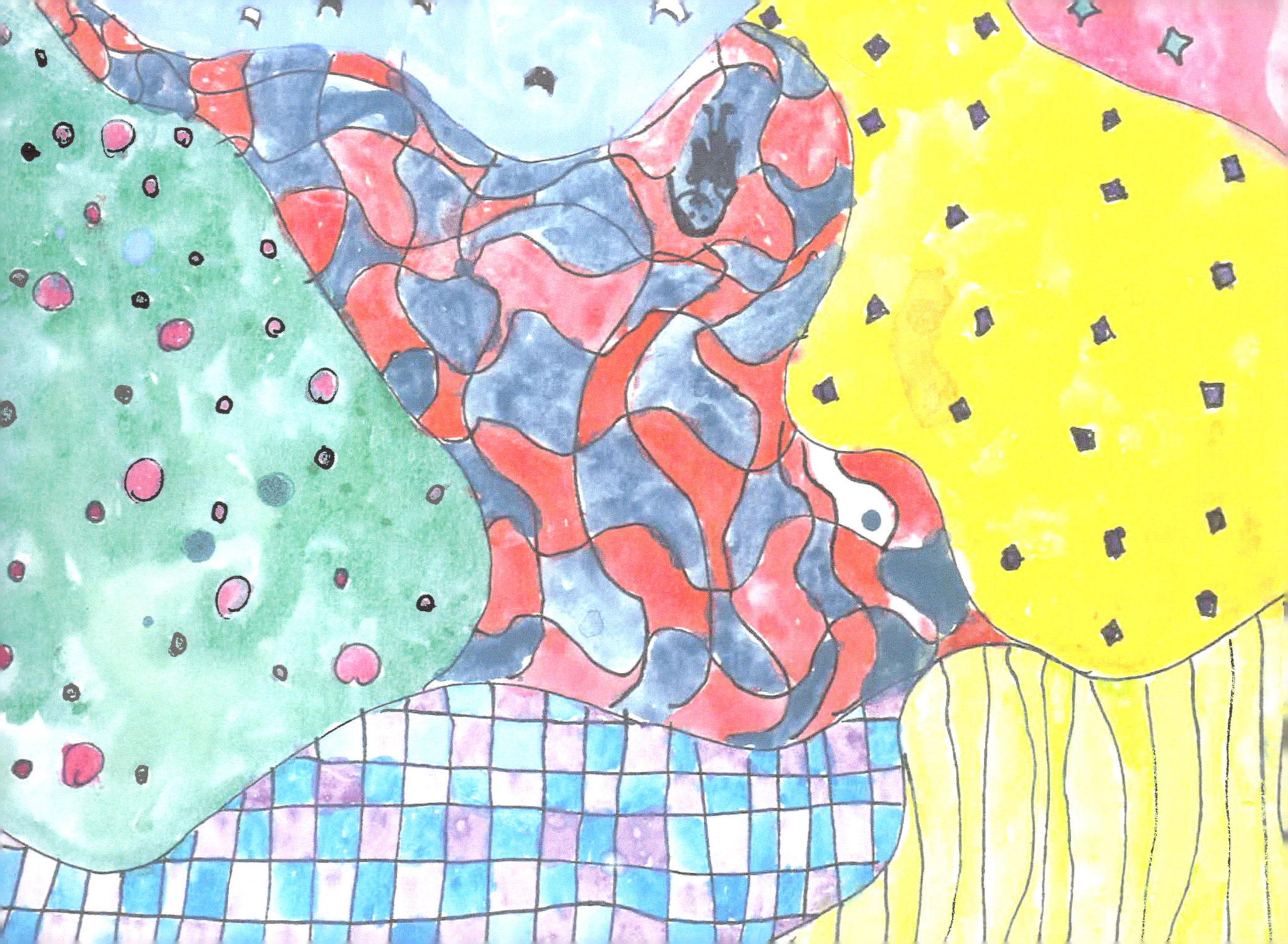

In my dream I am in a strange neighborhood wandering around. There were odd creatures peeking out from behind the surrounding waves and bumps and materializing on silent feet from the shadows. My new house was around here somewhere it had to be.

I looked up to see if it was day or night, I couldn't tell. The problem was the sky lookeded just like the road and walls around me curvy and colorful split into sections with each section a different design. Every once in a while a sun or moon

would appear then dissappear in a flash. Out of nowhere the street would turn into a skinny strip of ice or a soapy path. I kept walking...

by Maddie

In my dream   I saw a rainbow and I saw
a Unicorn and I rode away to where dreams
Come true and you got what you wanted!

By: Amelia

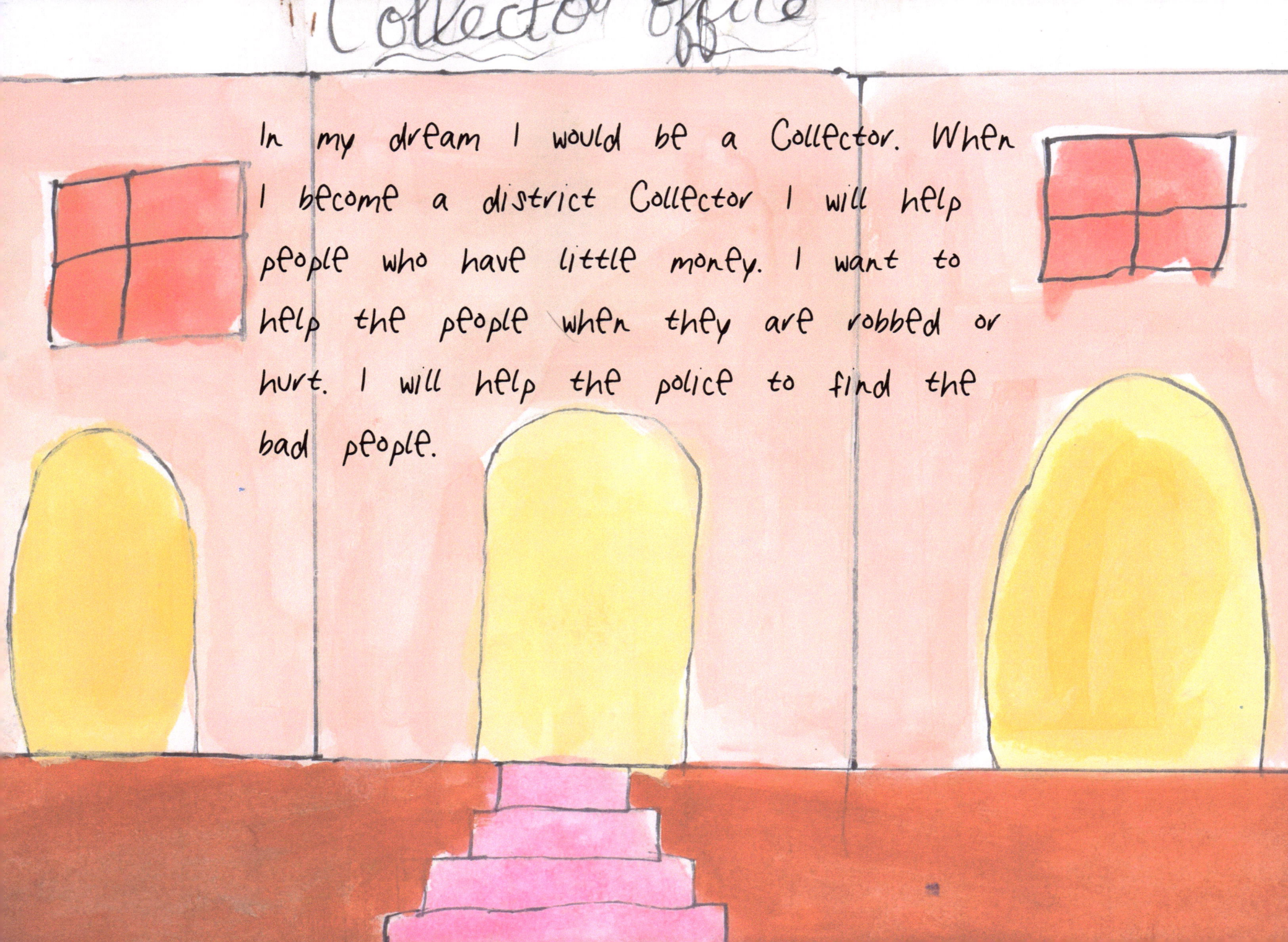

Collector office

In my dream I would be a Collector. When I become a district Collector I will help people who have little money. I want to help the people when they are robbed or hurt. I will help the police to find the bad people.

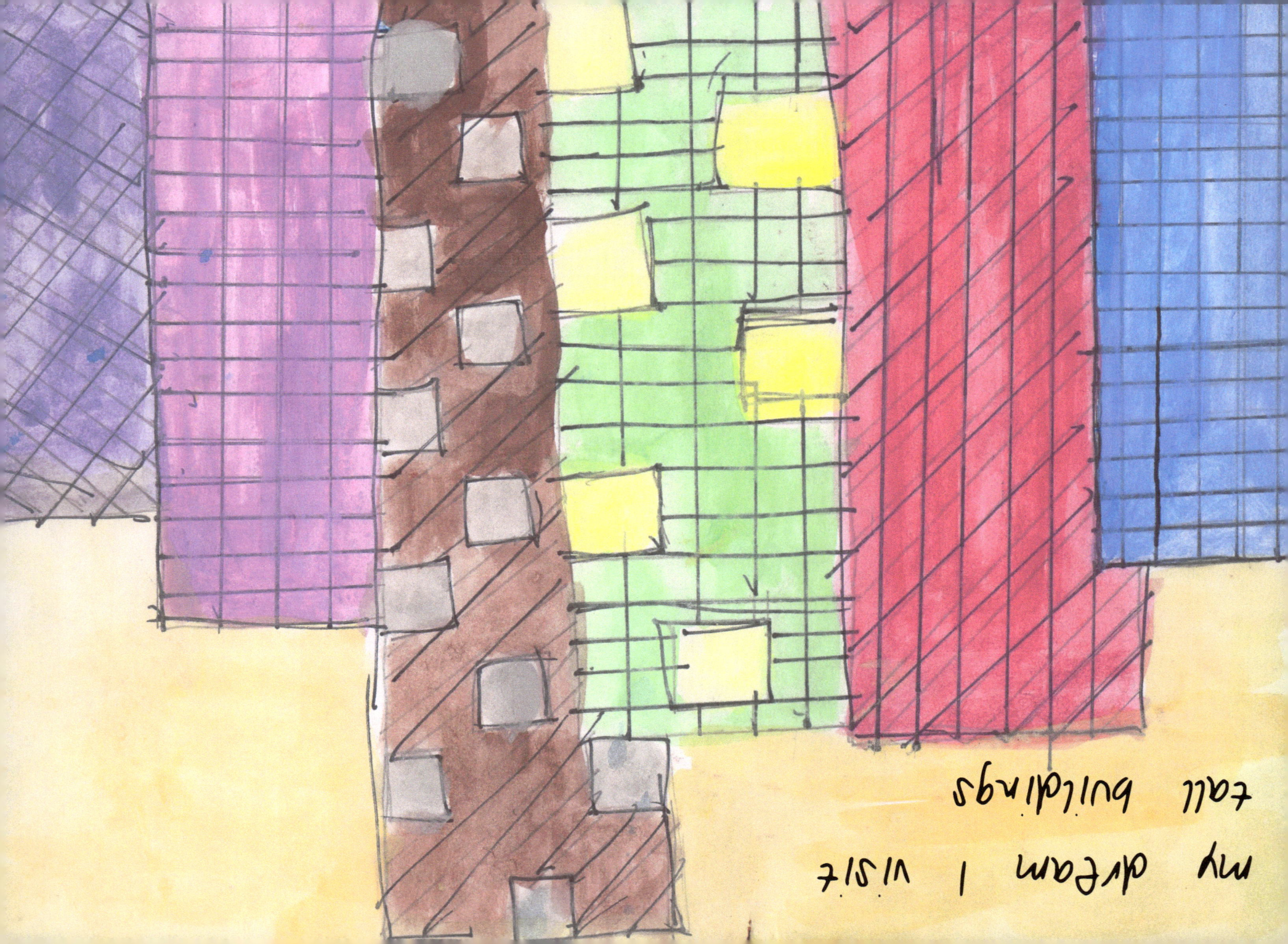

my dream I visit
tall buildings

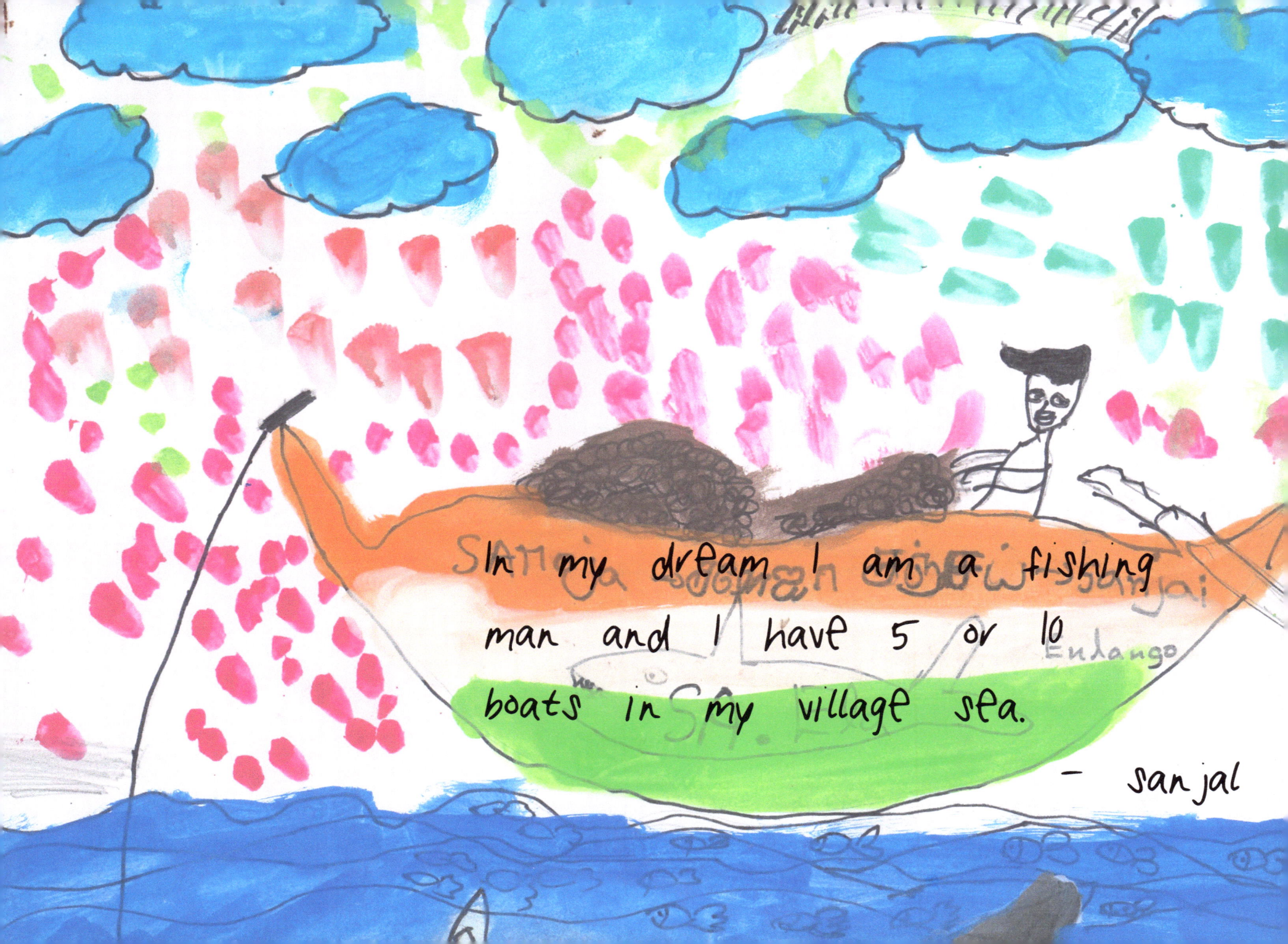

In my dream I am a fishing man and I have 5 or 10 boats in my village sea.

— sanjal

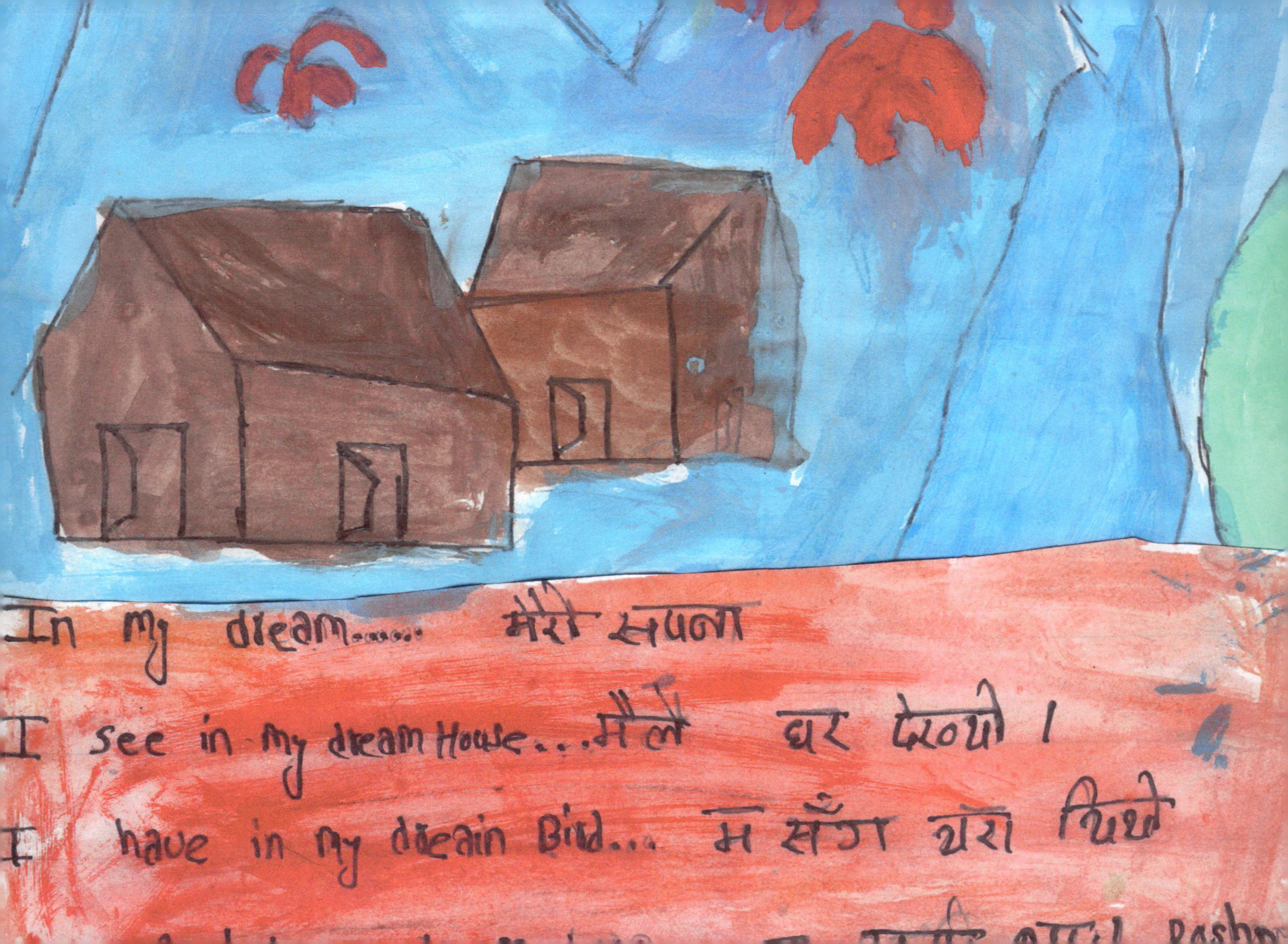

In my dream..... मेरो सपना

I see in my dream House...मैंले घर देख्यो ।

I have in my dream Bird... म सँग घरा भिषे

Rashm...

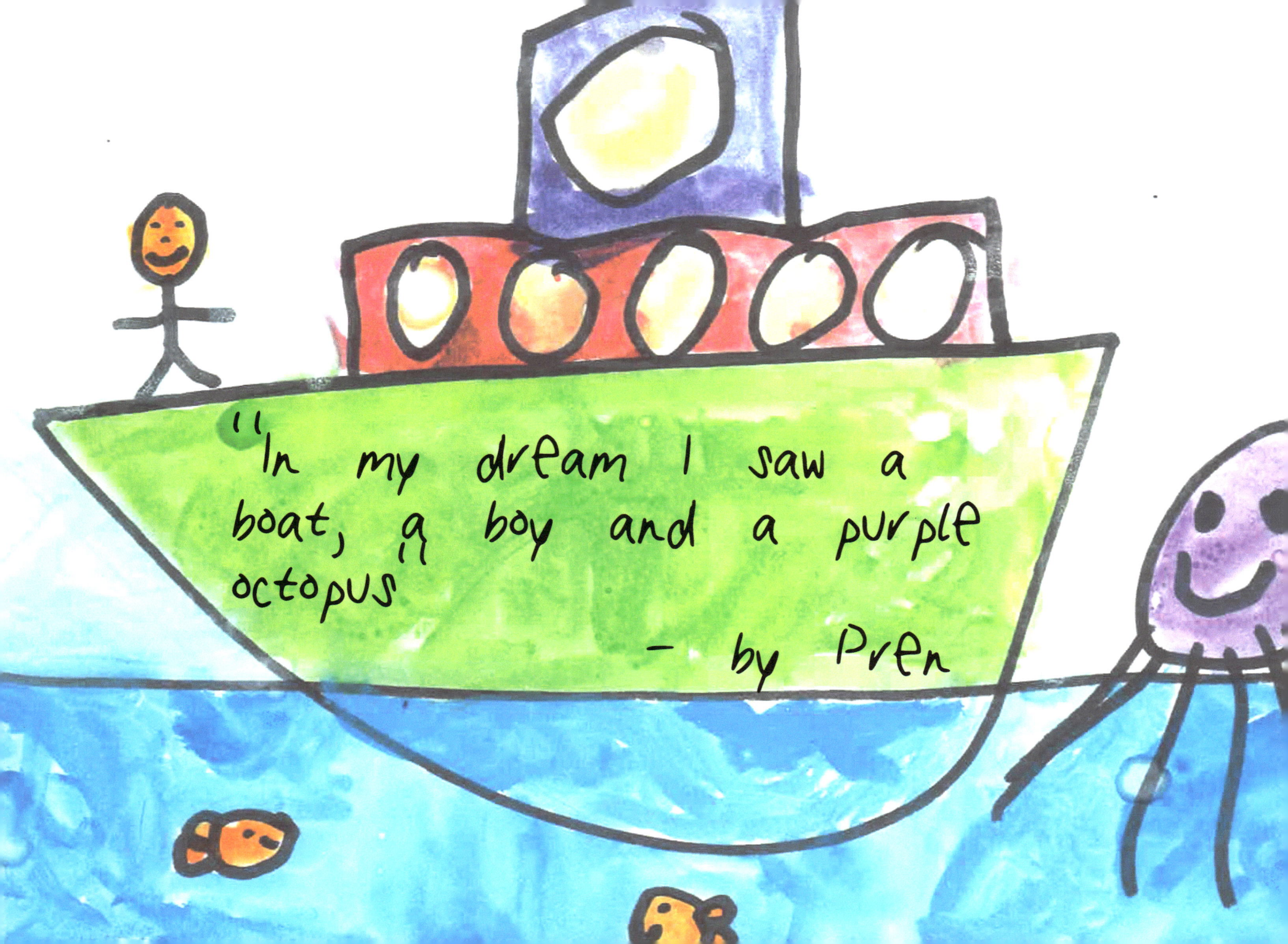

"In my dream I saw a boat, a boy and a purple octopus

— by Pren

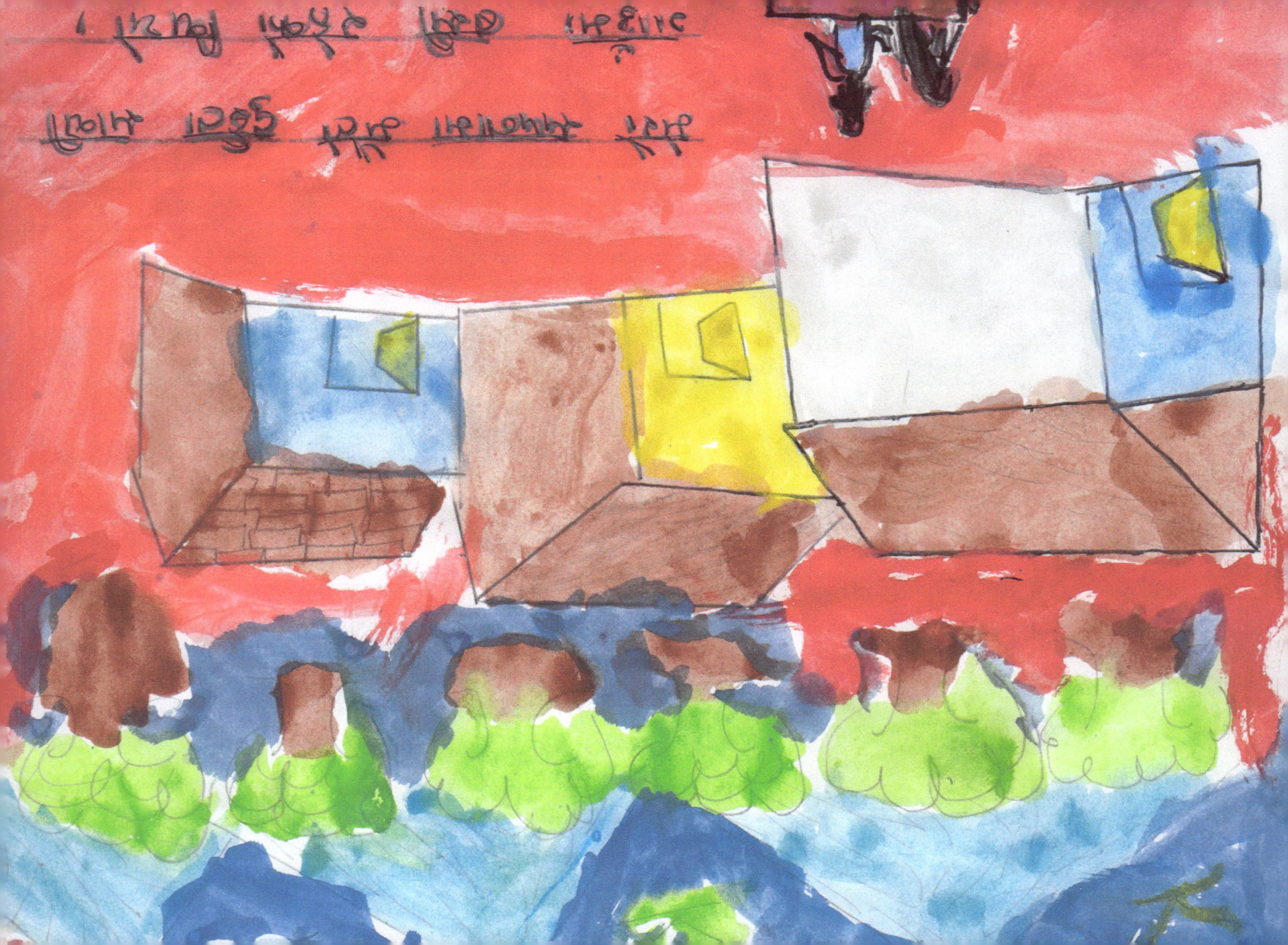

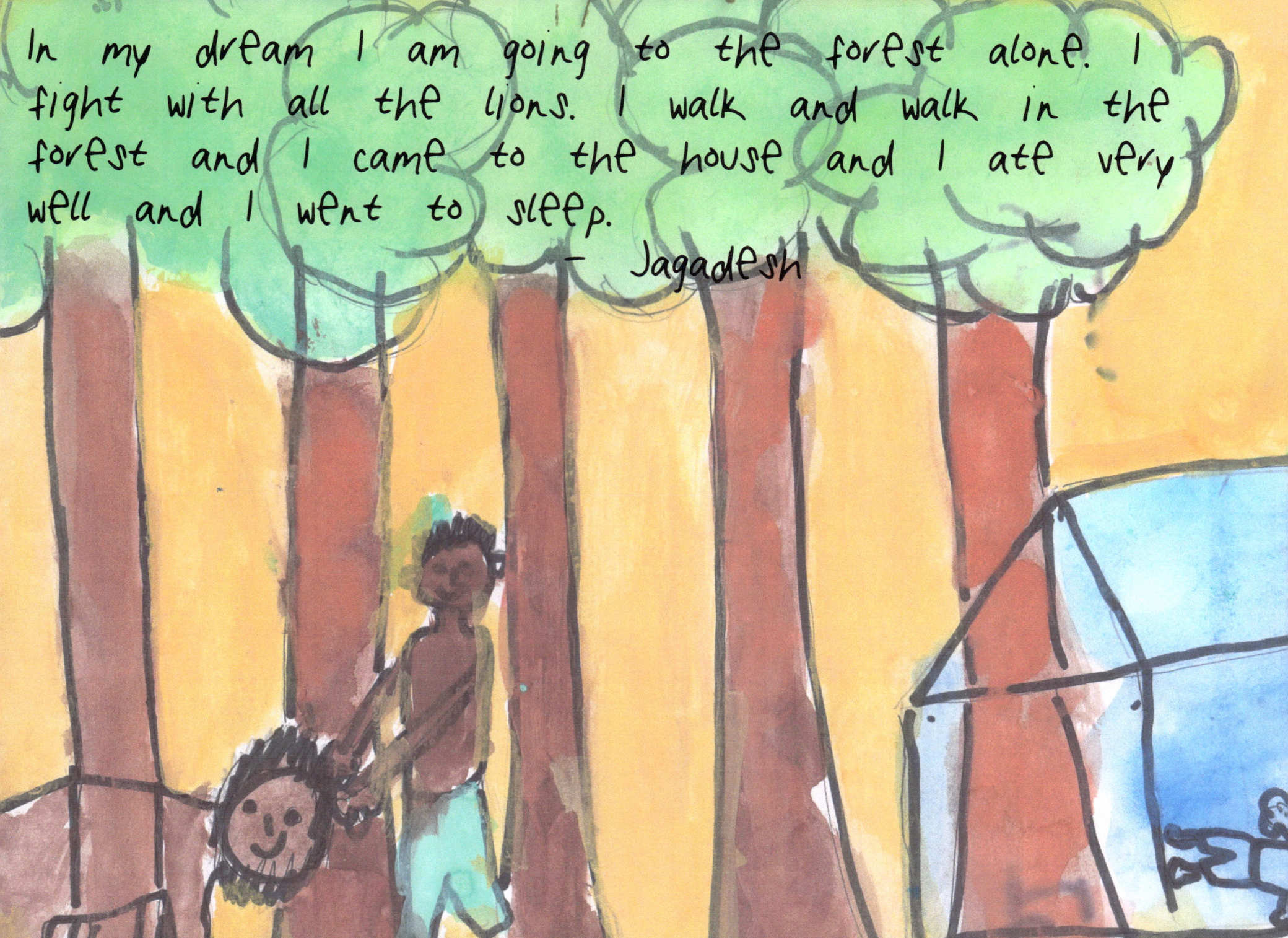

In my dream I am going to the forest alone. I fight with all the lions. I walk and walk in the forest and I came to the house and I ate very well and I went to sleep.
— Jagadesh

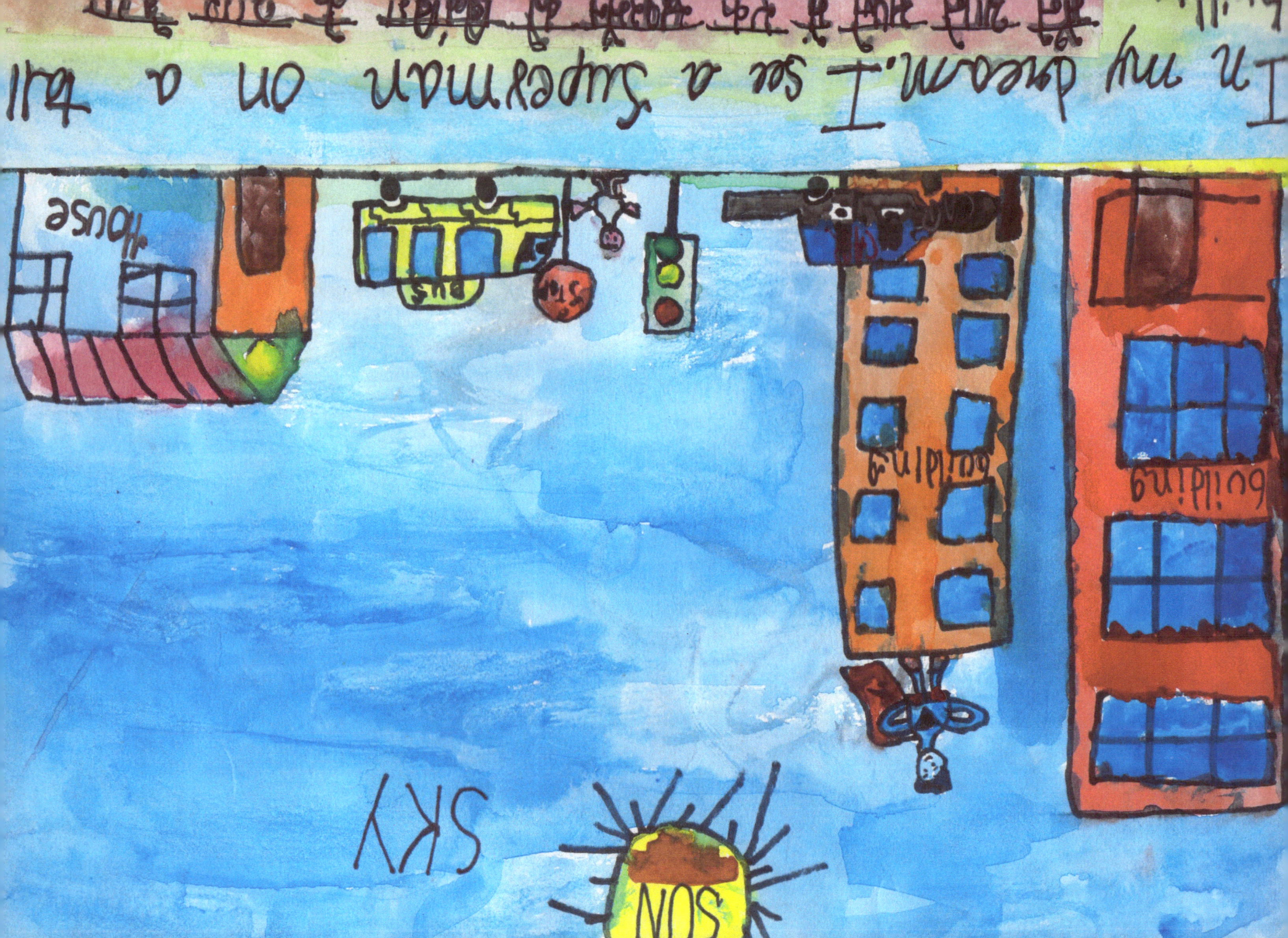

I saw my Dream is my new bat and ball.   Name-Divesh

मैने अपने अपने में देखा की मेरा नया बला और नीची ० बौल घी।

In my dream I thought the mountains were colorful.
They were green, brown, yellow and white.
The mountains were close by.

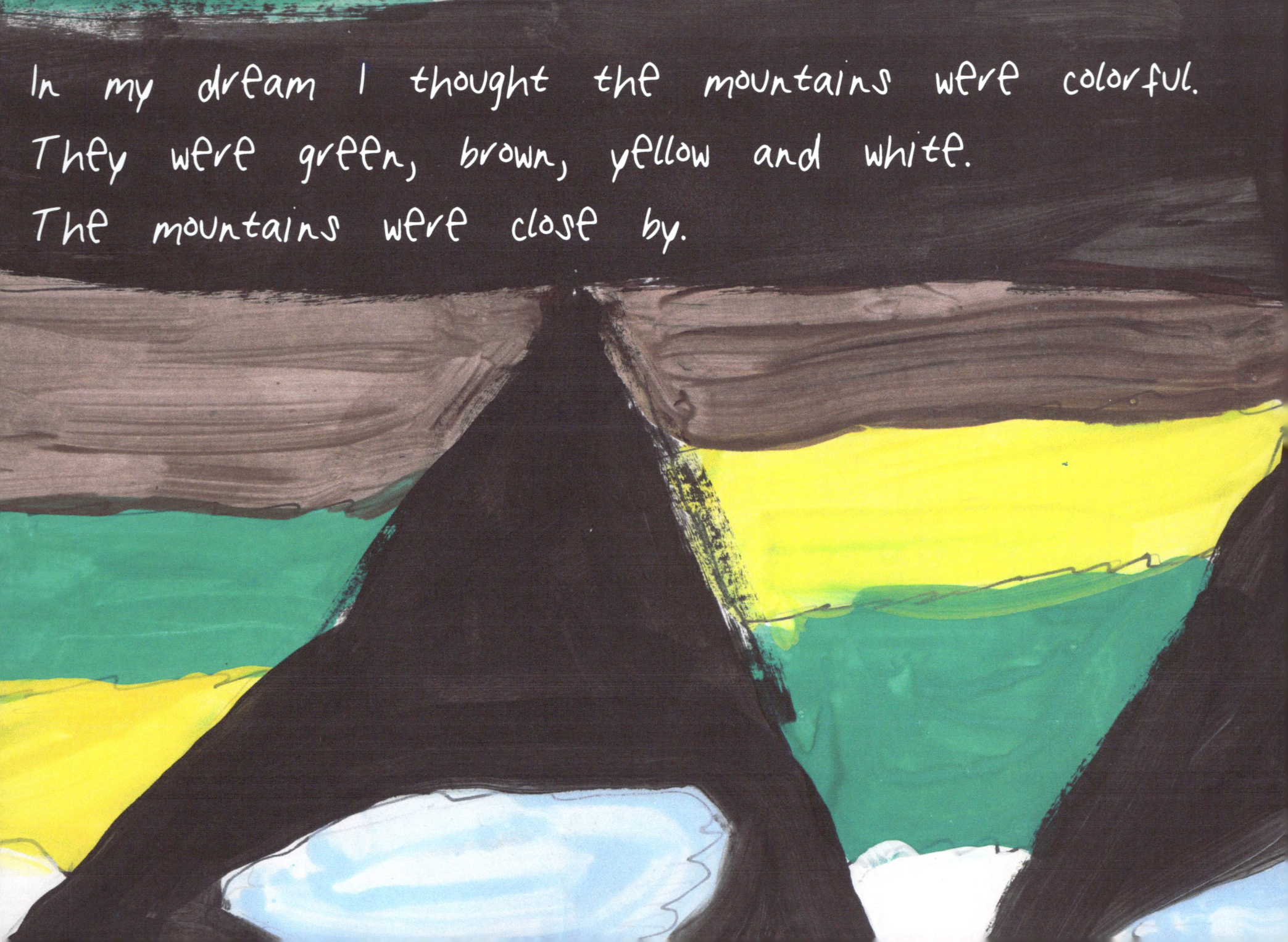

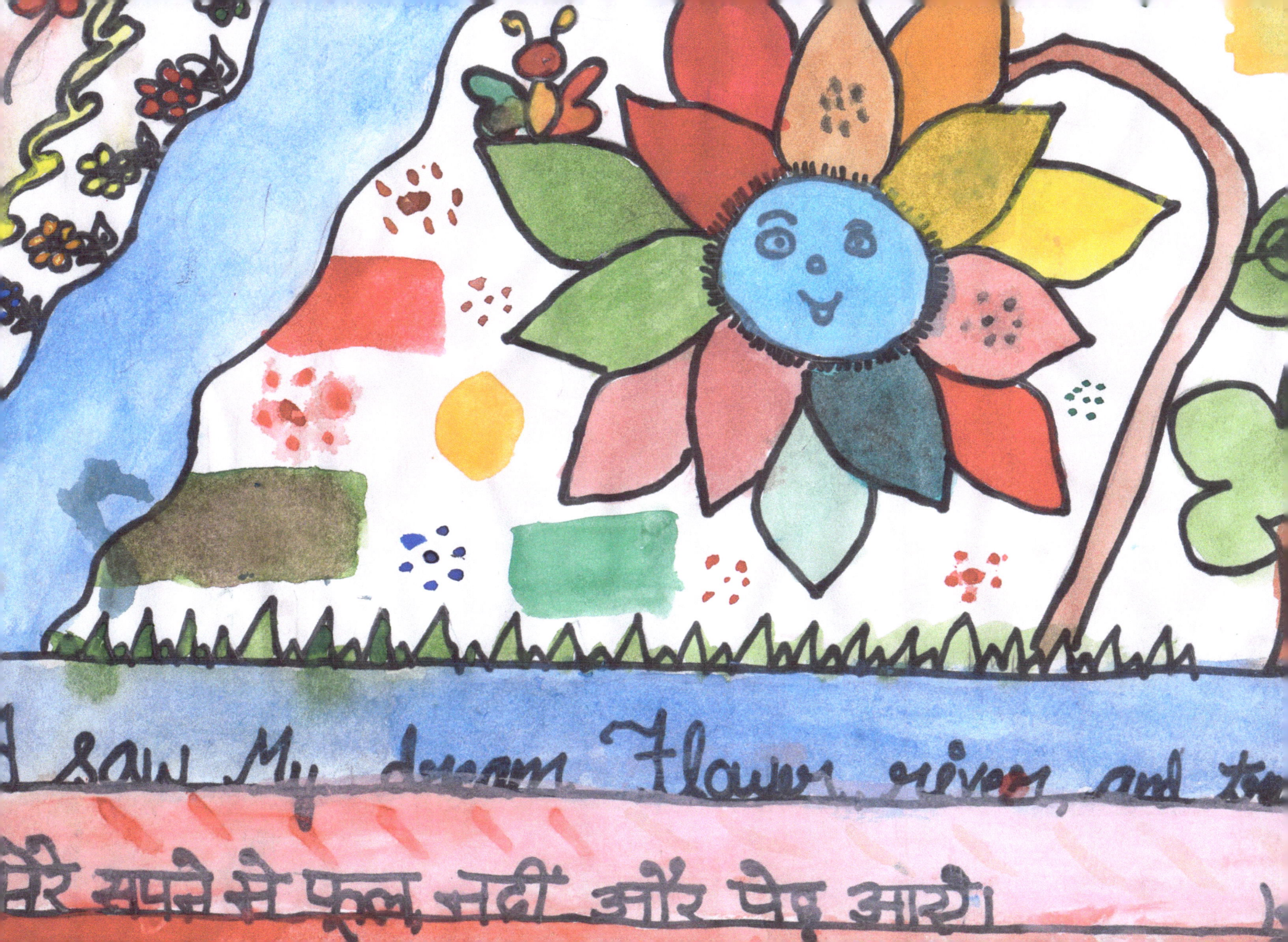

I saw My dream Flower, river, and t[...]

मेरे सपने मे फूल, नदी और पेड़ आये।

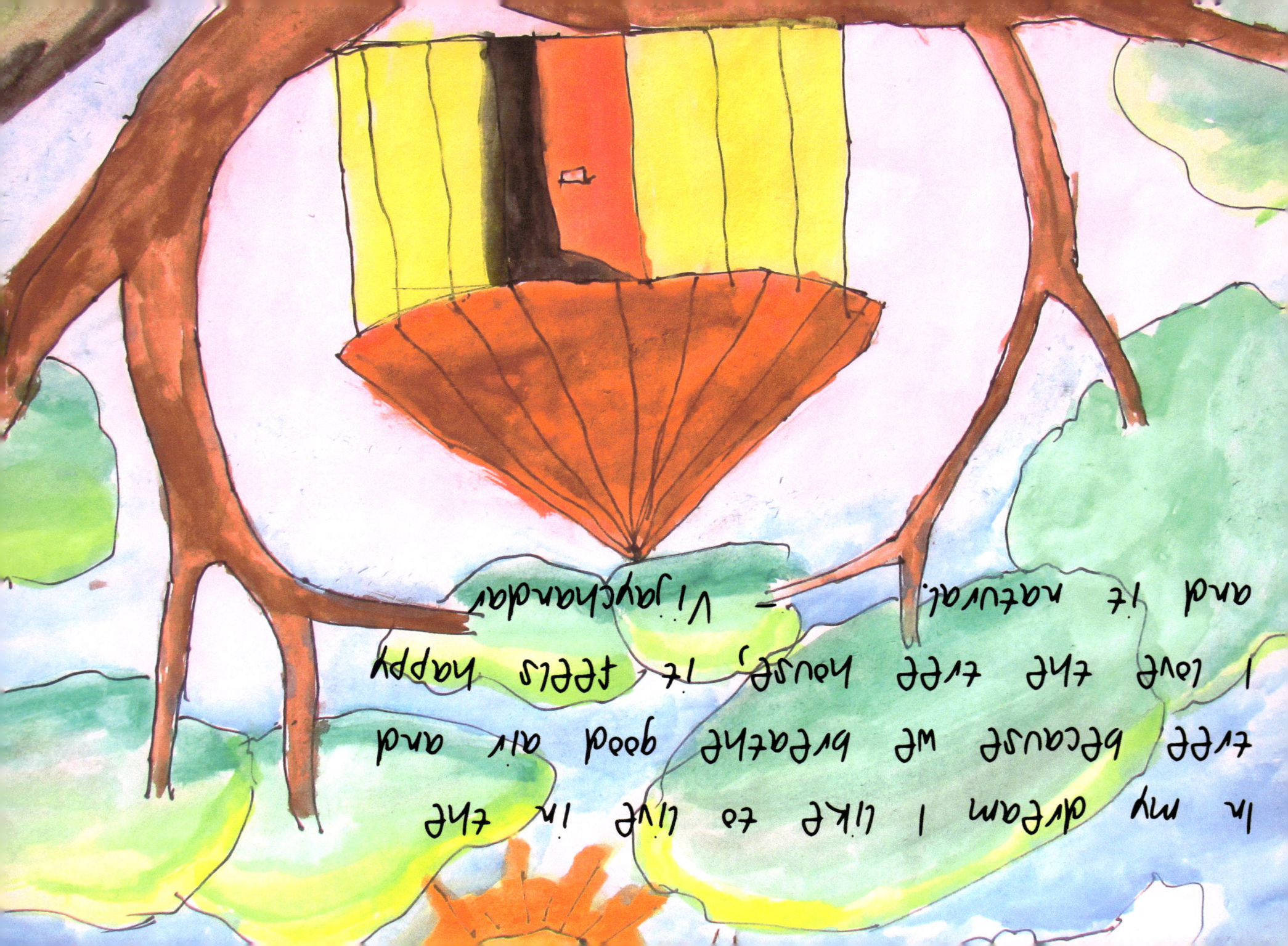

In my dream I like to live in the tree because we breathe good air and tree. I love the tree house, it feels happy and it natural. — Vijayachander.

In my dream I see a man tiger and me.

मेरो सपनामा Man Tiger देख र मेरो Man
Tiger को पछि सामान फालदेया

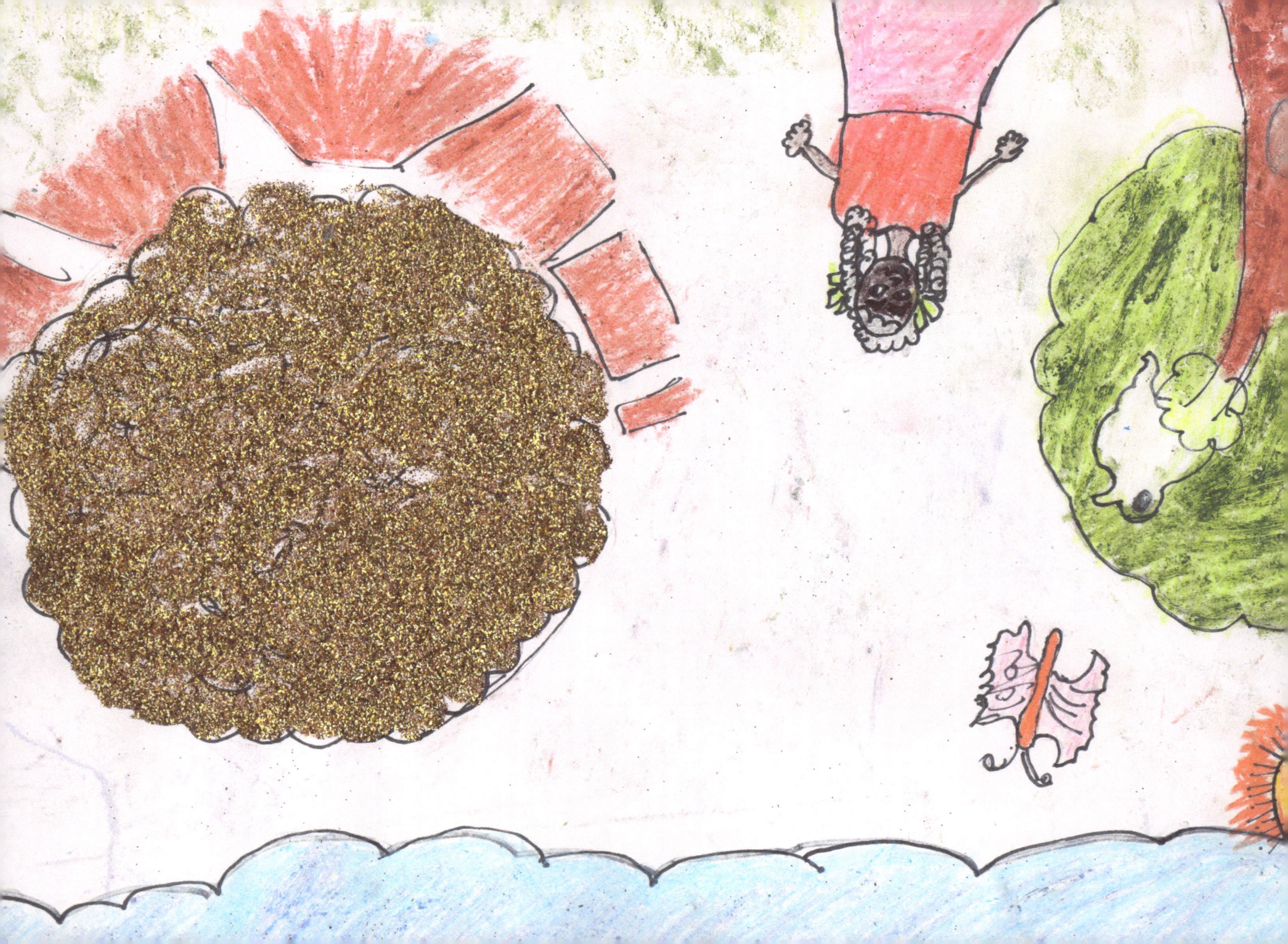

"In my dream I am going to the Matri Mandir. On the way I saw more variety of snakes and I saw more beautiful birds and colorful butterfly. When I went to the Matri Mandir, the thief came and they catchme and they took me to a cave and they asked me for money and I immediately ran. I go to Matri Mandir, I saw my parents and my family......and we live happily"

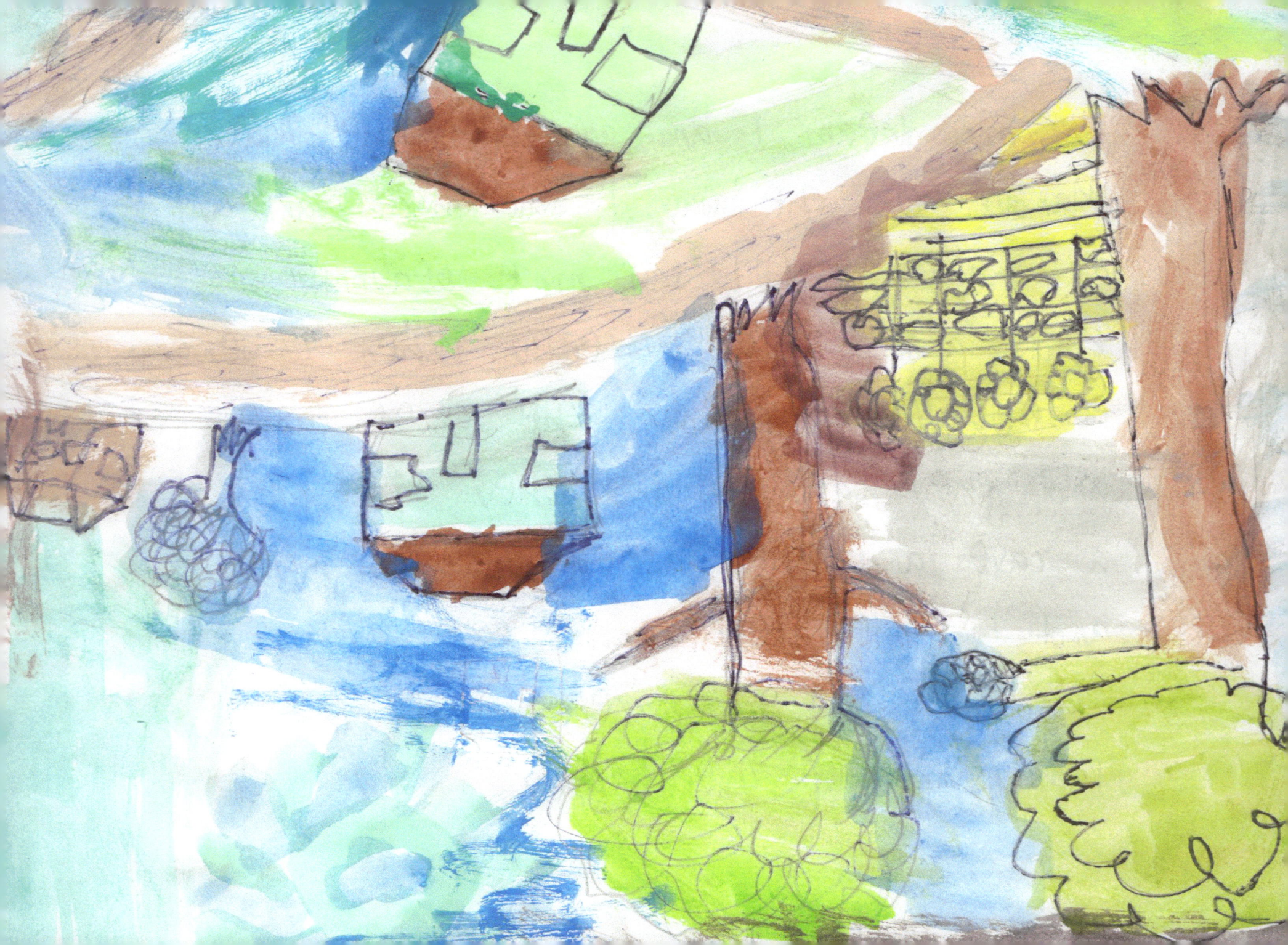

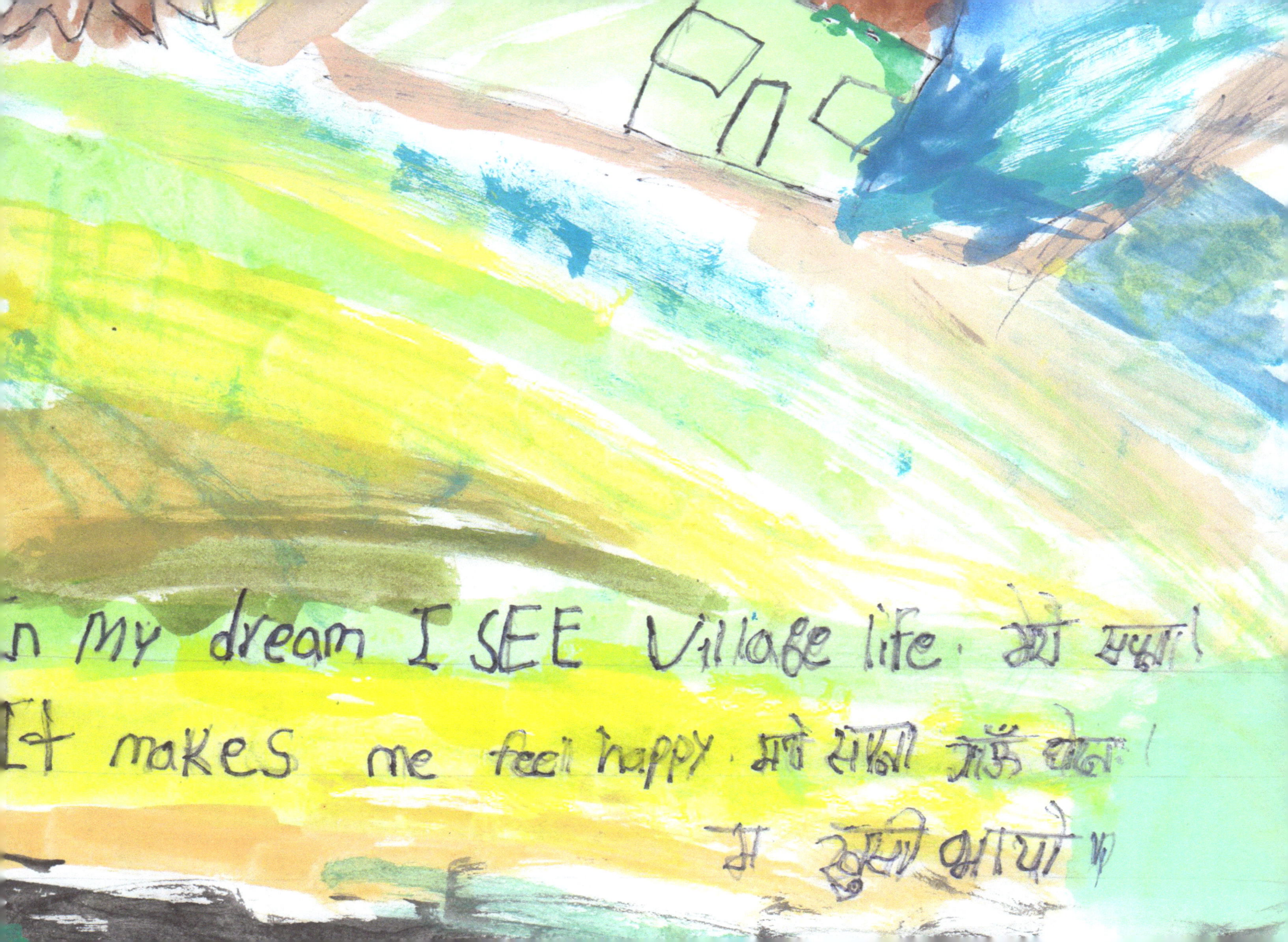

In My dream I SEE Village life. मेरो सपना।
It makes me feel happy. मलाई साथी राम्रो जेल।
म खुशी भायो॥

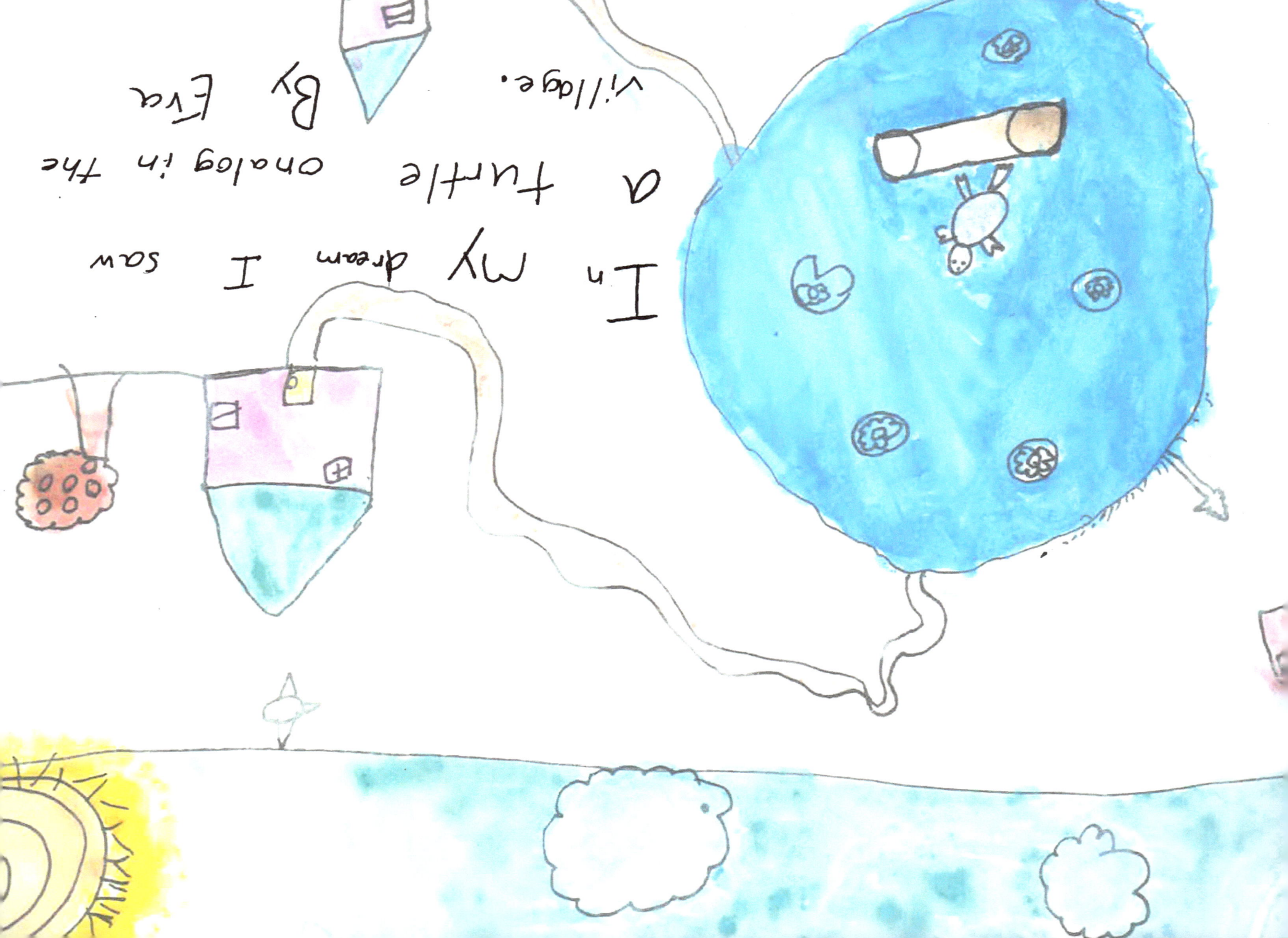

In my dream I saw a turtle onalog in the village. By Eva

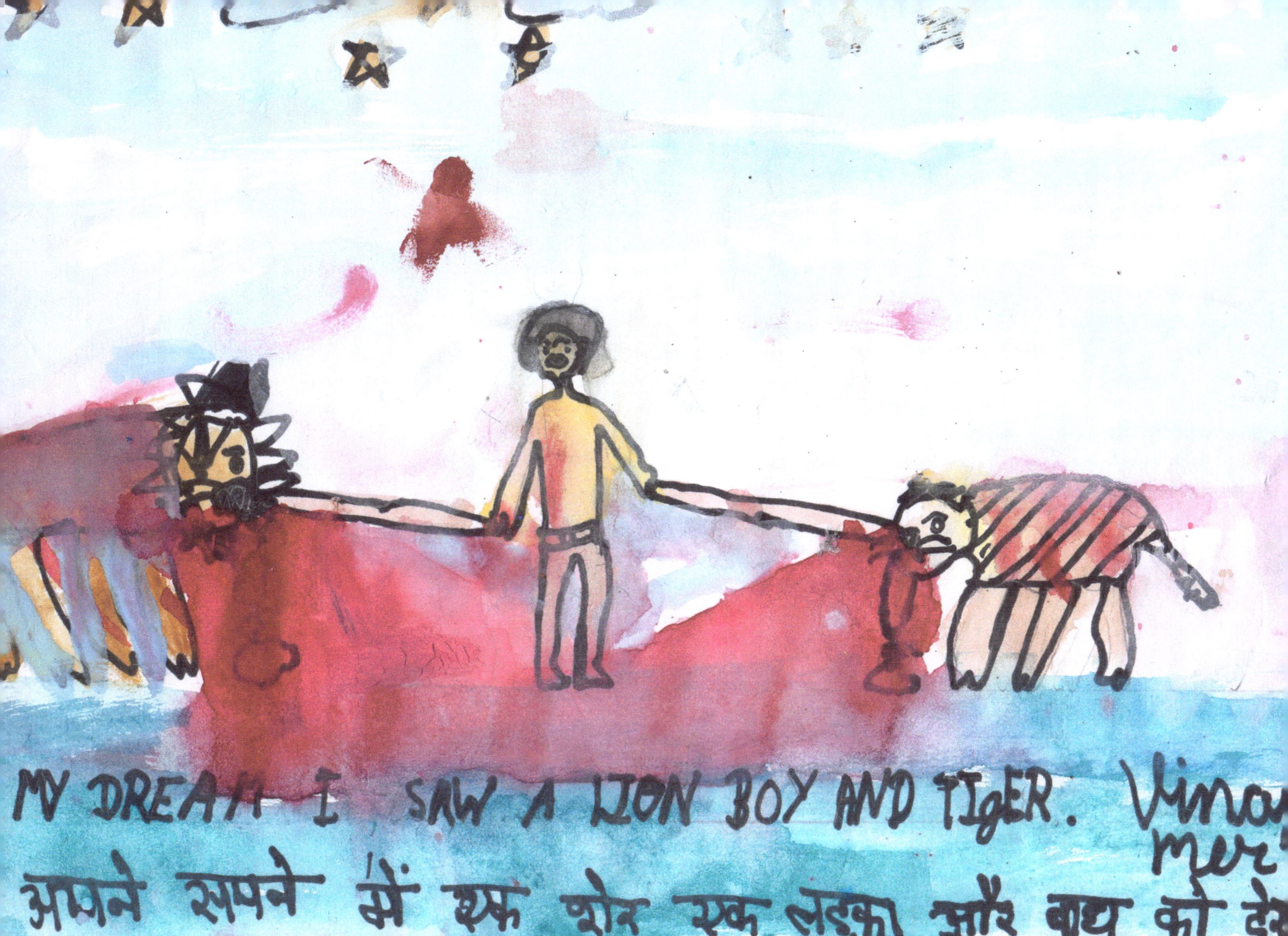

MY DREAM I SAW A LION BOY AND TIGER. Vino
mer'
अपने सपने में एक शोर एक लड़का और बाघ को दे

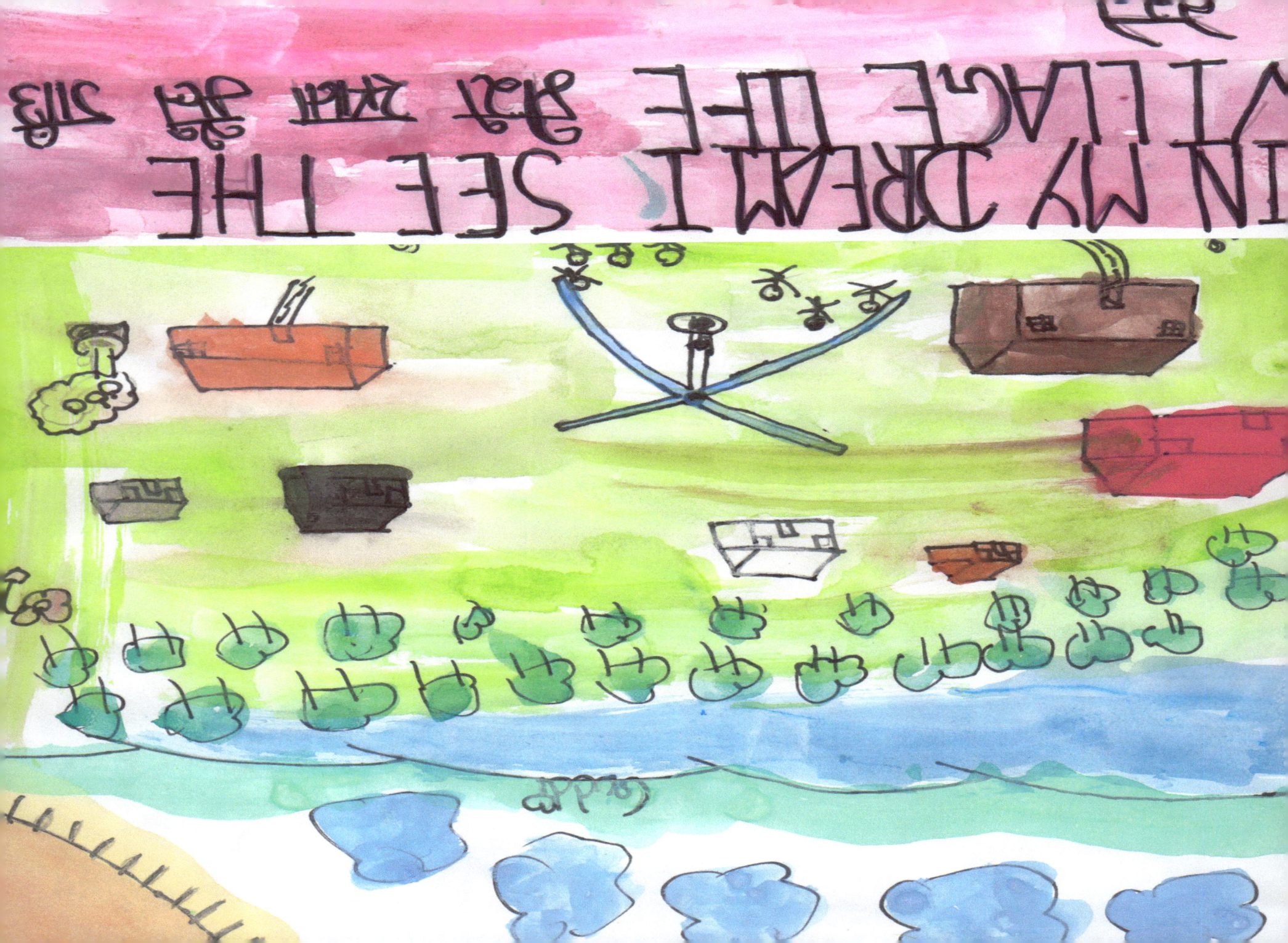

Acknowledgments

I would like to thank, with deep, heart-felt appreciation and gratitude…

 The families and especially the children of Salida, Colorado who have both supported and participated in Creative Playhouse, Peace of Art and Create and Transform programs for the past 18 years and for whom I have and will always have, an enormous PEACE of my heart.

 The students, teachers and Principal of Aikiyam School, Kuilapalayam, Auroville, South India… for the support and freedom provided to me and for the infinite creativity, boundless energy and imagination displayed by all the village children… especially, the first time authors and artists. Creating books by kids for kids was their idea, specifically of two young boys, who wanted to create an ABC Book for the youngest children to learn the alphabet. This is where Integral Art and Literacy came together to give birth to this wonderful project.

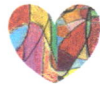 The Sri Aurobindo Ashram, Delhi Branch, New Delhi, India and Madhuban, Uttarakhand, North India whose Village Outreach program enabled me to guide and inspire both students and teachers according to the philosophy and practices of Integral Art (Integral Education and Art Therapy), in addition to providing the art space and materials that has enabled Village Voices to continue blooming.

 The students, teachers and Principal of Sunrise Public School, in Talla Ramgarh Uttarakhand… whose appreciation for art, creativity and the enhancement of social, emotional and intellectual development was always expressed with great enthusiasm and joy.

 Foundation for World Education… through funds provided by a grant which supports Integral Education, awarded to the Sri Aurobindo Ashram Delhi Branch, graphic design work on four Village Voices books was able to begin, in order to prepare for publishing.

 Anthea Guinness of Salt River Publishing who upon her very first and only encounter with Village Voices, embraced the project with open arms and a huge heart and provided fresh ideas, design, expansions and directions… www.saltriverpublishing.com

 Kartik Gera, graphic designer who is passionate about Children's Literature, is a pleasure to work with and has the patience to deal with my lack of technological skills.

BREAK THE TREND

A London publisher once said, "People will beg,
borrow or steal a book, but not buy."

Choose to be a buyer! Don't lend your copy to all your friends – order
two copies of this book **today** and give them away.

This is your chance to stand with all of us – the writers, artists, editors
and designers associated with the no-profit Salt River Publishing company.

www.SaltRiverPublishing.com
Publisher discount available at the estore

S A L T R I V E R

Salt River Publishing believes in encouraging artists and publishing professionals to come together and reach their empowered "Yes!"

Salt River was established as a no-profit publisher with the idea of helping writers, translators, poets, graphic artists and photographers bring their work into publishable form.

We provide links to a range of publishing professionals who offer services for anybody with a book in the making. And we publish books that inspire, encourage and entertain, including children's books and books that deepen the understanding of mysticism.

Do you have one?

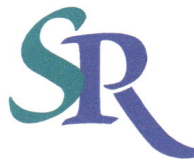

www.SaltRiverPublishing.com

READER RESPONSE
TO SALT RIVER BOOKS

"So many problems are spiritual in nature. And healing often involves finding meaning, purpose and spiritual uplift. The right words at the right time can turn a life around. Therapists and practitioners can point the way for clients who are seeking meaning; writers and artists have an opportunity to share in that work. Thank you, Salt River."